The Russian Revolution
By Robert H Wilde

History In An Afternoon 1

History In An Afternoon

1: The Russian Revolution

Contents

Introduction

People like to think that they, or others, can change history. That the ebb and flow, the course of events, are guided by human decisions, that we have some control. While there is a group of historians who argue that environmental and economic trends are really behind things, this book is going to argue that, at the start of 1917, an interplay of factors meant that the Russian Empire would experience a revolution. It will also argue that the year ending with Lenin and the Bolsheviks in charge was not inevitable. That, in fact, what we see in 1917 is a series of decisions taken by people which led to the replacement of an incompetent regime by, at the end, an outwardly murderous one. A series of decisions which went horribly, incrementally wrong. Decisions made by people.

A lot of ink has been spent discussing the inevitability (or not) of 1917, which is one reason this book provides a full context by starting the narrative in the 1880s, following Russia through one failed revolution and then two successful ones. Although, 'success' doesn't feel like the right word; that feels too positive. Orlando Figes chose the perfect title for his history: *A People's Tragedy*. But the answer to the old student question of 'why did 1917 happen?' is best understood by examining how Russia fluxed in the run-up to 1905, and then why things went differently in the run-up to 1917. The old human question of why did it all go so wrong is also best answered this way, and this book aims to combine the interests of both types of reader.

The Russian Revolution saw a dynasty which had ruled for hundreds of years not only fall from power, but be gathered and shot in a cellar. It saw a modern, liberal way of thinking wrestle with a world that was rapidly changing and fail, a blow for western thinkers who saw liberalism and democracy as inevitable. It saw the new methods of living— the cramped industrial cities—produce a new and partly mistaken ideology which a rising elite turned into a dictatorship.

World War One is the most important event of the twentieth century, because it caused most of what followed, including World War Two. The Russian Revolution is second, because it created the conditions which saw the USSR win World War Two and start the Cold War. It also allowed for a third of humanity to come under governments derived from what was established in Russia, a system that came to be known as communism, even though it bore little relation to a theoretical form of society that already bore the name. World War One birthed the Russian Revolution, in a collapsing Russia that had been pregnant for many years, and this child reformatted the world to such an extent that we are still dealing with it, years after the USSR vanished (although

6

Russian authoritarianism did not). Plenty of people will still tell you there is something in the Russian makeup that demands such authoritarian government, although it's unclear where the social studies of the issue turn into western bigotry.

But what is 1917? Most people think Russian Revolution, think Lenin, think Bolshevik, and given what happened, can you blame them? The Russian Revolution of 1917 began in February, when not one, but actually two revolutions happened at the same time, when liberals and socialists emerged from a revolt against the autocratic regime with a government each which competed, and then tried to work together. All the time they faced the same problems which crippled the previous ruler, the Tsar, and they could not solve those problems before many people, angry and searching for peace from the horrors of the Great War, welcomed a group untainted by compromise—the Bolsheviks, and their coup. That the Bolsheviks brought autocracy only became a factor far too late. Russian liberal democracy and social democracy were born, failed and died in less than a year, because something extreme offered quicker answers in a situation that, sadly, had very few, and which the first revolutionaries were not willing to take. It destroyed them. Throughout, the revolutionaries and ordinary people, had to deal with other forces let loose. Nationalism which caused parts of the Russian Empire to splinter. Raw human jealousy

7

caused peasants to turn on richer landowners with less consideration of Marx than anyone wanted to pretend was true. There was also the simple question of what on earth did any single, average person want to fight the First World War for?

If you want a quick way to understand the Bolsheviks, here is one: Throughout the events of 1917, the revolutionaries from all sides looked back at history, in particular the French Revolution. This was an explosion of tensions that transitioned from some of the most remarkable and hopeful days in history into a bloody, murderous Terror, and the Bolsheviks were actually happy to imagine they were the heirs of the Jacobins, the chief architects of this Terror. The Bolsheviks were a small group of highly eccentric and highly strung people who, thanks to years of exile, had only a tenuous grasp of the culture and life of the ordinary Russian (worker or peasant). They preached revolution but had very little idea of actual government, and were happy to start pogroms against the rich and the rebellious, providing they themselves were safe. They were able to both seize the moment and change the world, in the most horribly successful way. They are proof not only that people can alter the world, but that it's not always a good thing to let them do so.

The bulk of this book is a narrative history of the events that led up to, occurred during and were consequences of the Russian Revolution. I'm one of those people who believes history is best explained firstly as narrative, that this format spreads the information most efficiently, and with this underpinning people can go onto specialist discussions. This book is aimed at both students and general readers, so at the end of each chapter is what we used to call a crib sheet of all the main ideas from that section, although is now a tl:dr. The rest of the book is a series of vignettes looking more closely at key people and side events, serving as a hybrid narrative / textbook.

The aim of this book, and this series, is to allow readers to enjoy learning about the essentials of a historical event in a long afternoon. I love huge, detailed, often dry history books; this series is for people who don't. The subject might, and sometimes must, be serious, but the explanation can be enjoyable.

1: The Assassination of Liberal Russia?

A Murder

A carriage, driven along a regular route, on a day which should have been a celebration. A bomb, thrown at the carriage, which explodes and kills a guard riding with it. A pause, as the Tsar, the ruler and most powerful man in Russia, gets out of the armoured carriage to assess the situation, and is then wounded by a second bomber. If need be there was a third in the crowd. This was not the comedy of horrors which triggered World War One—that will come later in this book. This was the murder of Tsar Alexander II, the day liberal hope in Russia was fatally wounded along with him. It would take a good few decades to finally expire, snuffed out in the October Revolution of 1917. Had Alexander stayed in the carriage, he might have lived. Everything in history has empty possibilities.

The Great Reform

Alexander II is an unlikely liberal hero, because his 'liberalness' owes everything to comparison with the hardline conservative Tsars that followed. He was a man who came to the throne of Russia as the country faced humiliation in the Crimean War, and as you will see in this book, failure in war provokes reactions. The flashpoint led Alexander to believe, like many in Russia, that the war was lost because of Russia's weaknesses and reform was needed if Russia was ever to win a war again.

We're not talking minor reform here, like a new type of rifle for the soldiers. We are talking about Alexander II instigating the emancipation of the serfs (and yes, as you'll see, that was basically a con which left no one satisfied), creating a new level of local government called the zemstvo which encouraged local nobility and middle class members to run facilities like schools and repair infrastructure, a loosening of censorship, curbs on the church, and a whole raft of changes. The 1860s have been called the time of the Great Reform. It's worth spending some time with the zemstvos here because they will come up a lot. The idea to devolve some power down to a local level was at odds with the way Russia would then start trying to centralise it again, and there would soon be open verbal war between these sometimes well meaning, often very efficient bodies and a Tsarist system suspicious of anything that didn't do exactly as it was told. There was a new judicial system, enshrining concepts like trial by jury, and much more.

As you saw in that last paragraph, a book on the Russian Revolution can't even talk about something with such a happy name as the emancipation of the peasantry without explaining it was deeply flawed and a massive cause of what happened in 1917. Before the emancipation, peasants were basically slaves owned by the nobility, and they worked the land. After their emancipation ... they were free, but in massive debt, which meant they had no choice but to work the land or go to the city to join in with the desperate hunt for industrial jobs which could kill them quickly. Emancipation was such a massive moment in Russian history, but one that really was the most double edged of swords.

How could this be? Alexander was acting out of fear of losing international wars and local revolts, and yes, serfs were now free, but to have their land they had to cough up 'redemption payments' to cover the loss of the nobility, and these were charged at 6% interest over forty-nine years, which is a huge amount of time and money for a peasant who probably wouldn't even live that long. In the end, the payments were waived in 1907, but before that many peasants had to borrow to pay, and ended up in a debt as bad as serfdom. Nobody could invest in improving their land, even if they could afford to keep it. When they couldn't pay or when their new land was insufficient to provide for this accumulation of debt, peasants had to go to the noble landowners for paid work and still found themselves living like serfs.

The Russian population rose (Pipes cites an increase from 68 million in 1858 to 125 million in 1897) and you don't need to be an economist to understand why that put huge pressure on the land. In later chapters you'll see a lot of peasants demanding the land of the rich, and this wasn't just naked greed and jealousy, but the pressure of the growing population needing more land to survive on. Developments in farming stalled as the peasants couldn't invest, richer investors were sending their money to industrial projects like railways, and there wasn't enough free land to expand production. Landlords kept two thirds of the land, including most of the forests, whose wood peasants needed for warmth, cooking, shelter and food. It gets worse, because when we say they 'freed' the serfs, what we mean is 'from the nobility'. Peasants found they now had just as many legal obligations to the village communal elders, who could banish people and technically held the land which instead of the peasants. This situation was deliberately created by the government who were scared that a mass of free peasants might quit the land - where they were isolated and didn't show much desire to form mass revolutionary groups - to go the cities and cluster in rebellion, so made sure someone was still able to order them about.

At first, emancipation looked like it had worked as noble–peasant tensions reduced, but as the peasant population increased, land became scarce and money scarcer. The question of 'land reform', whether you want to class that as a

13

redistribution owed to the people or a land-grab from the rich, became a burning issue, *the* burning issue among Russia's population. As we shall see in 1905 and 1917, mass violence would follow, and when the Tsar fell the peasants expected land reform to take place, but the dual governments failed to tackle it in time.

Populists

The Populists (practitioners of Populism), are a group who sound like deluded proto-hippies until things turn very dark indeed. The terms are loose and cover lots of different groups, but essentially they were all revolutionaries who wanted to end the Tsarist autocracy, and thought the way forward was to idealise the Russian peasant communities. They believed the Industrial Revolution was dehumanizing, but thought if they acted now they could save Russia from the same fate, and promote the Russian village 'mir' governments. They were basically socialists in a time before Marx stitched that term up, focused on the 80% of Russia who were peasants rather than urban workers. They didn't want a capitalist stage leading to a socialist stage like later Menshevik socialists thought needed to happen; they wanted to skip all that and use the mir, save the mir, because it was perfect for socialist society. Rural socialists.

However, while peasants were genuinely illiterate, poor and lived in houses architecture calls vernacular but everyone else calls rough, the Populists were upper and middle class, educated and moneyed. You can guess where this is going.

The Populists believed in 'going to the people', which meant the rich teaching the poor about revolution, and in 1873-4 Russia saw a remarkably strange period when an almost religious belief in the power of their conversion skills led Populists to travel to peasant villages and try to educate. It had no overall leadership, varied by region, and utterly failed. The peasants weren't happy at being saved, as they saw these Populists as suspicious, soft dreamers with no idea what village life was like. In some areas, Populists were even arrested by the peasants and handed over to the police.

That might be a funny story were it not for what happened next. Populists who returned home were disappointed, and some were even radicalized as they tried to turn their anger at this failure (and belief the peasantry couldn't save themselves so the revolutionaries would have to do it for them) into something else. Many became Marxists, because it was new and interesting, but many others turned to terrorism in order to trigger change (and many became both). Terrorism increased in the 1870s, not because of a mass movement but because a tiny group of people fell in love with violence, managed to perform a string of terrorist acts which took on a life of their own, terrifying the government, until a Populist offshoot called The People's Will (there were only 400 of them in total, and the practical part was a few dozen) managed to get agents to bomb Alexander II. As we've seen, he was killed. After this, Alexander III brought repression, and the Populists turned into other groups, some of which studied this terrorism with interest.

Four ex-populists (George Plekhanov, Paul Axelrod, Leo Deutsch and Vera Zasulich) formed a new group called the Group for the Liberation of Labour, the first Russian Marxist society. Naturally, it couldn't be formed in oppressively policed Russia, so was founded in Switzerland.

What Died With Alexander?

This book will try and be unflinchingly honest, and so we can't explain that Alexander II tried these changes without also explaining that he was an essentially authoritarian man who saw his reforms start to fail, and that they produced such a reaction, ran into such problems, you can argue they were already failing before his death. King Henry V of England died just at the right time to be forever considered a success, moments before things were about to go wrong. Alexander II died just at the right time to look like the assassination of liberal Russia, but things might have been about to go wrong. Yet he tried, they happened, and on the day of his death he approved a series of reforms which, while not the creation of a parliament or a constitution, were a step on the road to them, a step he acknowledged. This era was not perfect, it was messy and hard, as any reform tends to be, but for many it was a time of liberal hope. Of possibility.

This was what died with Alexander II: the idea of compromise. The People's Will, a group of terrorists descended from a group of idealists, triggered a massive repression, and you can understand why the next tsar wasn't that keen on the direction Alexander II had taken seeing as it killed him. The next tsar, Alexander III, fought back with repression and authoritarianism (which he was very good at), turning Russia into a police state. Indeed, Soviet Russia is famous now for the brutal, secret police paranoia and rule of Stalin, and Lenin before him. What people do not realise is that system originated here, under Alexander III, as the legal system was subverted by the government and as the very fertile roots of the police state grew. The horrors of the Gestapo and the Cheka and NKVD were prefigured. An example: from 1878 on, an armed opposition (not necessarily an actual terrorist attack) to the government would be tried under military law using courts martial.

Equally, you could be punished and exiled for simply being suspected of opposing the government. You didn't need to have actually done anything, just upset the wrong person and you were arrested. The old secret police were reformatted, and in their place Russia received two simultaneous police forces, one for the public, and one for the state and the Tsar. The latter didn't give a hoot what the former thought was sensible law. Let's zoom in on perhaps the most understandable example: for many jobs, for instance, working at a university, you had to acquire a certificate of trustworthiness from the police, whose sole criteria for granting them was their opinion of you. If you weren't keen on university life, you needed permission to start a Sunday school or publish a journal. Most histories call the Russia of Alexander III an autocratic monarchy, but Richard Pipes, a keen historian of Soviet history and no fan at all of it, calls this era a proto-police state, the father of what the Bolsheviks had. They didn't invent their system, they used what was already developing. It wasn't that Russia didn't have a constitution, they just didn't have a liberal one, instead they had a police charter which governed a century of their history. That the system was badly run, clearly counterproductive and out of all proportion didn't matter. What mattered was your average unhappy Russian couldn't find a political voice without being led into the world of revolution. Such was the broad brush scale of the repression, that in early 1917 just about every opposition voice managed to come together against the Tsar.

In turn we come to Nicholas II, the man thrown out of power by the Russian Revolutions of 1917. He was the direct heir to a fear of giving an inch to the people, to democracy, to any concession at all, partly because of what happened to his ancestor, who lived long enough to be carried back to a palace but was too badly mutilated to be saved.

Nobody knew when Alexander perished that this would be the high watermark of reform in Russia for over a century. The liberals still hoped to effect change, still hoped to convince first the Tsar, and then the people. Nobody had known the Western Roman Empire had ended either when it had. The sad truth was that the terrorists couldn't have helped Alexander III and his counter-reform supporters any more if they'd signed up for him instead.

CRIB

- The Crimean War was a disaster for Russia and made people want reform.

- New Tsar Alexander II delivered the 'Great Reform', emancipating serfs, creating zemstvos and trying to bring Russia forward to meet challenges of rival European nations.

- The emancipation of the serfs was basically a con, and only reduced tensions in the short term. Fault lines soon began to grow.

19

- The Populists failed in their ill-conceived attempt to 'convert' peasants into revolutionaries, and some turned to terrorism in anger.

- Alexander II's changes faced stiff opposition, and he was assassinated. His reforms mostly died with him.

- The terrorists only succeeded in helping the authoritarian counter-reformers.

- The next Tsar was a counter-revolutionary who tried to turn the clock back several centuries.

2: Russia in a Changing World

The Famine

An event occurred in 1890s Russia which cries out to be the start of any dramatically minded narrative, so easy is it to load with meaning and foretelling. We'll get to it in a minute, because something more important happened first, in 1891. Orlando Figes' 1990s history of the Russian Revolution starts in the same place as this, but I suspect he didn't realise that so much of the twenty first century would be affected by the same thing: a drought, and a famine. Just as Syria collapsed into civil war and birthed ISIS because of a drought, in 1891 terrible weather caused a famine which would snowball into great change, albeit over a longer period.

Russia was a vast empire stretching from the now independent Poland, all the way through Asia. In the west ran the Volga river, the longest waterway in Europe, and this region was affected: bad frosts, bad spring, no rain in summer. Water vanished, crops failed, people started to starve. As with Syria, and any famine, people did not sit around and wait to die; they started to move in search of food, of life. They ate anything they could, including bark. An area of thirty-six million people suffered. Diseases like typhus and cholera followed. Hundreds of thousands of people died.

The government tried to react, but faced some serious issues: it was a ponderous bureaucracy that could not and did not rush decisions, attempting to organise an underdeveloped and backward transport system into taking action. The system failed, and contributed to people starving. However, not only did the government fail, but it was seen to fail: people began to blame the government and the civil service. An area where food didn't arrive would accuse the government of corruption and evil rather than simple institutional stupidity, so it wasn't just that the Tsar and his ministers had failed, but they had failed terribly and cruelly.

Then the government really did do something terrible and cruel. A proposed ban on cereal exports was delayed, and enough notice given for anyone with lots of grain to send it quickly abroad and take the money. Not only did the government ignore the situation, they made it worse, and were also seen to. Given the government also refused to talk of famine and use muddled words like 'poor harvest', you can see how the Tsarist elite earned a reputation of being not only uncaring, but being in a conspiracy, that the famine was only so bad because of the Tsar and his actions.

Russia Gains Consciousness

You might be thinking, this is a book about the Russian Revolution, do people revolt now? And no, not yet. There was no 1891 or 1892 rebellion like 1905 and 1917, but Figes started here because something vital did happen. Very few people wake up one day as revolutionaries. Something has to happen to change minds, and in Russia in 1891 the liberal class began to change. Why? The government, which wasn't really involved in an evil conspiracy, decided it needed help and on November 17th 1891 called for civilians to organise public, charitable relief for the starving.

People responded in numbers, in sweat and blood. From workers who donated what they could to aristocrats desperate to alleviate guilt, people came together to help. Kitchens were organized to provide food, medical teams went out, hundreds of little groups of people formed to provide all the care and supplies the nation's starving needed. Leading the way were the zemstvos, rural committees created in the 1860s by a liberal Tsar to help society, and they used their little networks like never before. One of them, the Tula zemstvo, was led by Prince Lvov, a man who will feature greatly in this narrative, a man who only ever meant well and was ground down by politics. At this stage, he was a ball of burning energy, like so much of Russia. There were other names, and I mean people who will feature in centuries of history: Chekov and Tolstoy, writers who worked tirelessly to aid the hungry.

So why did this matter? After all, the zemstvos were created in the 1860s... The Tsar's call to the people, and their response, went far beyond the intended goal. The Tsar wanted the hungry fed, but suddenly an entire class of people in Russia organized, looked at the world, reached out to change it, and realized they could have a say. There was a moment in the French Revolution when a class of lawyers and similar people looked at the chance to complain to the government, to be elected to the Estates General, and realized 'we have a voice'. Russian Revolution experienced it too, here, a key moment in the development of a political consciousness among liberal Russians. It did not cause an instant revolution, but as you'll see, it snowballed.

Tolstoy turned his work against the government, castigating the Tsar, the old fashioned social structure and the Orthodox Church as being to blame for the mass deaths. Given that the church banned peasants from taking Tolstoy's food after they'd excommunicated him, you can see why he was annoyed.

The famine passed, the crisis ended, but the politicized liberals of Russia did not go back into their bottles. They had seen the failure of the state, and they had seen their own success, so of course they wanted a say in how the country was run, not just on theoretical principles like democracy, but because they had seen themselves do it better. Journals roared complaints, committees met, people kept pushing and pushing. A liberal Russian opposition was forming against the Tsar.

The Socialists

It wasn't just liberals. Socialism had experienced a down period in the 1880s in Russia, but with people organising and discussing, it roared back again. It wasn't just the return of an earlier ideology called Populism—now there was a new idea in socialist thinking: Marxism. These groups will be discussed more in the next chapter, but in essence Marx promised an application of scientific theory to moral hope, and although basically wrong it found easy appeal with people who wanted the new fad, the new way of reacting to their guilt and jealousy. Socialist beliefs grew to the extent that a law graduate called Victor Chernov could become leader of the Socialist Revolutionary Party, which was founded in 1901. Unlike Hitler's use of the term, this group pretty much wanted what the name described. At this point both Marxists and Populists accepted that workers and peasants were united in opposition to the Tsarist regime. But it was the famine that caused so many people to turn to Marx, including the hordes of students and teachers and committees who saw it as the only answer to the famine's cause and prevention. The hunger gave Marx a way in. One young man, a socialist of a different creed, converted to Marx as a direct result: he was called Lenin, and he would rule Russia by the end of 1917. But what happened with Lenin and the early

25

socialists is so fundamental to this story it will get its own chapter.

Reform The Tsar, Not Replacement

Russian society had changed, from the radicalized workers and politicized liberals, to the reaction of the old elites against them. Russia was changing, and fault lines had crystallized. This change had been happening before 1871, but this was the tipping point. It's at this point in a history book where we have to talk about less obvious forces at work. Industrialization, cultural change, social breakdown, all were taking place as the modern world was birthed. What did this mean for revolution? Education was opening up, and more people were enjoying the benefits, meaning more people to talk in the new political culture. Social mobility was increasing, meaning peasant offspring could become upper class. There might not have been a British-style middle class, but there was a broader change in the fabric of society.

People didn't want the Tsar to be a God-given ruler with sole power. People turned away, to look at the idea of Russian people leading their own Russian state, although the nature of this changed between liberal and socialist. Their leaders were the leaders of an experiment unleashed in the 1860s which came of age in the 1890s, the zemstvo members. These were not socialist firebrands wanting terror, this was not

1918. The leaders of the zemstvos were elite, noble, landowning, but also liberal, enlightened and concerned. They were royalists who didn't want to remove the Tsar (at this point), but wanted to act as consultants, ideally in a government assembly, which would help the Tsar reform himself and help his people.

This might seem innocent enough. The Tsar could work with natural supporters wanting a bit more attention. The liberals didn't yet want to remove him. As you'll see many times in this book, a chance for peace and a little reform was ignored by the Tsar and turned into such a disaster it alienated people into opposition and finally rebellion. The Russian Ministry of the Interior actually attacked the zemstvos, considering their minor opposition dangerous and radical, using arrests, censorship and finance before the famine to hold them back. The politicization of the famine led to even more active zemstvos, ones calling for national organization and a national assembly, which the government once more tried to harm. Secret groups of zemstvo men, including Prince Lvov, formed to campaign against their persecution, and for a new constitution. Not without the Tsar, but a fair one with him.

So far, so peaceful. But there was violence too. Students and other people were radical, as they always had been, and formed cells which would conduct acts of violence and terror, assassinating government officials among others. In return, demonstrations were put down with military violence.

Nicholas II Starts Badly

Then Russia got a new tsar. The previous one, Alexander III, was a backwards-looking autocrat, but he had the advantage of being quite good at it. The new one, his son, had been written off by Alexander as useless and never properly schooled in how to run a nation such as Russia. When Alexander died in 1894, Nicholas II found himself Tsar and was properly terrified. If he wanted something to boost his confidence he got the opposite, because the days after his coronation were a disaster that looks like I've made it up to foretell the revolutions.

It was a few days after the coronation ceremony, and just outside Moscow was Khodynka Field, a patch of military land with trenches and defences and all sorts of obstacles. A celebration had been organized here for ordinary people and, promised food and gifts in the form of tankards, beer and massive meat dishes, half a million of them came to see what would happen. Unfortunately, a rumour spread that there weren't enough presents for everyone and the crowd surged in a rush to get what there was. The field wasn't flat, and soon people were crushed underfoot, in trenches and ditches, and others suffocated. Fourteen hundred people died. The Tsar

28

then showed exactly what he thought of the tragedy by allowing himself to be talked into carrying on as if nothing had happened, including holding / attending the French Ambassador's Ball that night.

Public opinion was outraged at this slight, and Nicholas, not totally tone deaf, appointed a former Minister of Justice to punish the people responsible. The nobility / integrity of this aim evaporated when he discovered it was not ✓ only a Grand Duke, not only a Governor-General of Moscow, but also the Tsarina's brother-in-law, and the matter was swept under a particularly threadbare carpet. Nicholas, and a lot of his critics, would look back at this as an omen.

It's important to take a moment here and look at what was happening. A society where the Tsar had been seen to fail, ✓ while liberal and socialist opposition competed with each other and the government. You will see this again, but at this point everything was more moderate than later. And just as you will also see again, a war broke out which caused an attempt at revolution.

1904-5: A War Pressures Everything − Sino-Russian War

The 1904-5 war between Russia and Japan isn't given much attention in the West anymore, and usually only as a byword for spectacular and embarrassing failure, which it was. It is essentially what happens when a racist government operating at the far reaches of a long supply chain run into an efficient, active and rising nation. We'll give it some time here— the Baltic fleet story is well worth it.

In 1860, expansionist Russians named a settlement on the Sea of Japan Vladivostok, which sounds typically Russian to Western ears, but which actually means 'Rule the East', just in case anyone local was in any doubt what the Russians were doing there. Over centuries Russia had expanded and kept expanding, but with the military powers of Prussia, Austria-Hungary and the Ottoman Empire, which was refusing to die, Russia's hunger for more turned evermore east. Alaska might have been sold to the US, but this wasn't a step back, just the feeling it would be too hard to defend. Closer land was still wanted. The locals included not just China, but a new version of Japan. If that seems a strange way to talk about a country with a long and proud history, Japan had, for several centuries, isolated itself, and only after 1855 did it turn back to the world and modernise itself to compete. Prussian instructors and admirals trained in Britain's Royal Navy all helped Japan roar back into the great game of international politics. Russia going east, Japan looking west, a clash was inevitable.

In the 1890s, Japan fought China and won territory on the mainland and control of Korea through a friendly government, but lost it again when Russia and other European powers, who were all meddling in Asia to build their own empires, acted. Japan was hugely embarrassed, especially when Russia in effect took all this land and control for itself. Russia was left with land very close to central Japan, which they could use to mount an invasion of this state, and the latter wanted to use as a landing post into the mainland. Russia felt the expansion was going well, while Japan readied itself for a reckoning and a war.

Japan was a modern military, full of Prussian zeal and loyalty to the emperor. They were the sort of organization that would map in detail the areas where they might be fighting. Whereas Russia, distracted building railways across Manchuria, didn't really bother, and was too busy turning the Boxer Rebellion of 1900 into a Russian occupation of Manchuria to consider having to fight Japan over it. Japan worked politically, and gained the support of Britain and America. By 1902 Russia was meant to be slowly withdrawing from Manchuria, but the government was divided, and ended up trying an imperialist charge into the region. That this collapsed through ineptitude wasn't significant; it was that it convinced the Japanese that if they did not fight Russia now, on the mainland, Russia would come to conquer Japan. The latter knew they had an advantage in the area, and a quick victory would be needed before Russia could use the vast and rickety supply line from European Russia to the east.

Russia wasn't just stretched out on a supply line and poorly organized. It was also massively racist, considering the Japanese to be 'yellow monkeys' who couldn't fight properly. Very few people in Russia had taken the time to study the Japanese and their military, and those who had were concerned, but the Tsar and his leading men thought any battle with the Japanese would be won by racial superiority as much as tactics. It wasn't just centuries of expansion, it wasn't just businessmen telling the Tsar to attack in the East for their own profit. It wasn't just that European neighbours were encouraging the Tsar to fight the 'yellow people' to move his focus away from them. It was that the Tsar considered himself an expert on the East who quite fancied being the conqueror of huge new tranches of it. History and world politics played a role in the Russo–Japanese war, but Tsar Nicholas II's fingerprints were on it. They were normally sticky.

In February 1904, Japan attacked the Russian fleet at Port Arthur. They didn't score a war-winning attack, or anything close, but they inflicted a dent in morale, with Russia appearing disorganized, badly equipped and confused. The Japanese looked in control of events, and they were. Russia's immediate counter to this was the morale-boosting order for Vice-Admiral Makarov to take over; Japan's immediate counter was the morale-shattering killing of Makarov in his badly thought-out attack. The Japanese now landed at Port Arthur, and were soon advancing.

The Russian commander, General Kuropatkin, assessed the situation, and as he was one of the few Russians who appreciated what Japan could do, he planned to be on the defensive until the thin supply line provided numerical superiority, something Japan could not match. The commanders below him, on the ground, had different ideas about what was needed, and weren't afraid to ignore orders for glory. Or, as it turned out, a lot of death.

Japan's land forces engaged Russia's, and they started winning. This brought morale boosts, strategic gains and foreign investment for the former, while the latter were weak, under supplied and not sure what was happening. Port Arthur held out, but the Russians in charge of it were arguing. Around it, Japan was squeezing. Kuropatkin was losing the arguments and attacks to relieve Port Arthur failed. It was not a walk over (accidents at sea robbed Japan of siege guns and vital trains, amongst others), but as war raged, and supply lines bit deep into both, the trend was one of Japanese professionalism and Russian laxity, and Japan was winning battles at sea and on land. Not that the Japanese assaults on Port Arthur were working.

When Kuropatkin did get his numerical superiority, his intelligence was so bad he didn't realise and stayed defensive, while the Japanese were so skilled in gathering data and so bold that they attacked anyway. A close-run battle followed and the Russians withdrew. The year progressed with more battles, and Russia sent another army. Kuropatkin was claiming victories he hadn't won, the Tsar was going along with it to please the public in European Russia, and Kuropatkin was given even more power. When winter came, both sides needed the rest, but battle did not stop at the siege of Port Arthur. After nearly a year, on January 1st, 1905, with the command inside still arguing, the Russians surrendered and the signature was given the next day.

The Battle of Mukden came early in the fighting season of 1905, and when Japan won, pushing Russia back, Kuropatkin was sacked from command, and at his request demoted to a unit. We now need to pop back briefly to 1904, for the start of one of military history's most ridiculous stories. With the Russian fleet in the east experiencing major difficulties, the Second Pacific Squadron was formed … from ships in the Baltic, which you already know is actually the opposite side of Russia. The plan was to outfit this force, and sail it all the way round to the warzone, a journey of eighteen thousand nautical miles. The cavalry would be coming from far away, and the logistics were enormous—not least of which was the question of how to carry / source the coal to fuel it. A journey filled with mutiny, disease, arguments over coal and plenty more problems took seven and a half months. It ended when the Japanese worked out where the Russians were aiming for, engaged in the Battle of Tsushima, a comprehensive Japanese victory which saw the whole Russian unit destroyed or surrendered, and caused a crushing blow to morale. You can't sail a fleet halfway round the world, lose it in one battle, and pretend that things aren't an utter disaster. To say the Tsar looked silly is an understatement (the commanders who surrendered this fleet were later sentenced to death, but 'mercifully' given just life imprisonment by the Tsar).

Russia had already experienced marches, riots and an abortive revolution. The Tsar, finally facing up to reality, became convinced the war had to end. Japan needed it to, as they were dangerously stretched. Peace negotiations took place, and Russia came away with a much better settlement than they might have expected by pointing out they still had a huge army. Japan agreed because they were exhausted. But in Russia, to the people of St. Petersburg and Moscow, that didn't matter. Humiliation and defeat did.

Japan began to believe it was a naturally gifted nation that could vanquish larger enemies and win a great empire, a belief that would burn half the world in the 1930s and 40s. But that is for another book.

Liberal Hope and Hurt

The new organizations of the 1860s and 90s had offered to help the Tsar during the war, and the zemstvos, led by Lvov, gained permission to organise nationally and send a medical brigade. It was a watershed. But when the war went terribly the political Russian people reacted, and their initial support of the Tsar turned into opposition. Liberals criticized the Tsar, while extreme socialists took a harder line, which included blowing up the Minister of the Interior, Plehve, a man who had allowed the war and was so unpopular hardly anyone cared he'd just been vaporized. Calls went out to form what, many thought, was a perfectly reasonable demand: a national zemstvo assembly. Plehve had always blocked it, but the Tsar seemed to be responding to the crisis by listening and appointing a self-styled zemstvo leader to the open job: Prince Mirsky.

The liberals demanded more representation. The socialists too. Mirsky was receptive and tried to persuade the Tsar. But Nicholas II, brought up an autocrat, refused any limitation on his power and the two sides rubbed against each other. The friction would, in 1905, bring about an attempt at revolution. At first, in late 1904, Mirsky thought he'd organized a zemstvo assembly that would hold back and stay subdued, and when he realized they wanted to talk about new parliaments he tried to deflect them by allowing one meeting for a cup of tea. That's not me being cute, he really did allow a meeting for tea. The zemstvo assembly met from November 6th to 9th 1904, with 103 members. Lvov was a vice-chairman. It wasn't a secret, and large sections of Russian society celebrated their first national assembly. Mirsky took their demands to the Tsar, he looked at them, and rejected them. His concessions avoided all the central issues. There was to be no assembly.

Then a revolution began in St Petersburg. You could skip to chapter five to read that, but chapter two is vitally important to understand how all this went very wrong.

CRIB

- A famine in the early 1890s was a disaster for the people of Russia, but also highlighted government failings.

- The government reacted by calling on the wealthier people to help. They did, becoming connected and politicized as a result. A new consciousness appeared in Russia.

- This consciousness included a liberal intelligentsia, and a socialist mindset split between frustrated workers and almost dilettante revolutionaries.

- Many liberals wanted to keep the Tsar as part of a constitutional government. Many angry poor turned to violence to effect any change at all.

- Russia then got a new Tsar, the poorly educated and poorly equipped Nicholas II. He was an autocrat who wanted to go backwards when it came to reform.

- What the Tsar did want to do was win a colonial war in Asia to feel superior, and a combination of racism and arrogance (and okay, stupidity) caused a complete disaster in the Russo–Japanese War of 1904-5.

- The liberals were asked to help, and did so, but in return asked for a national zemstvo assembly. The Tsar reacted by ignoring them.

- The failure of the war and of reform triggered an attempt at revolution in 1905.

3: The Bolsheviks and Mensheviks
(aka How Tantrums Changed the World)

A Terrible Lesson

This book is going to mention socialists a lot, because they were a massive force in the revolutions of 1917 and some of them won the struggle and took control of Russia. But socialism in Russia in this period, as in the entire world, was not one monolithic thing. Like any ideology, it was broken into fragments, each with competing ideas and egos which usually didn't get on with each other. What is odd about socialism was how petty some of these factions became, falling out over obscure points of ideology most other people would ignore in favour of getting on with the revolution.

In one sense, the subject of this chapter deserves being separated out because the origins of the Bolsheviks, the socialist faction who would 'win' in 1917, is so important you have to see the birth. That's how most books pitch it. But there's another reason this book has been structured like this, and it's to draw your attention to the fact that the Bolsheviks were born out of a moment of petulance, and how that would be repeated several times over the years, and things would get worse each time. The tantrums of the Bolsheviks' enemies opened a door they ended up marching through. This chapter isn't just about how the Bolsheviks were born; it's about the fact that just because an act of clear stupidity has happened before doesn't mean it won't keep happening until people are locked in camps.

A Broken Tile

If I told you Lenin, who ended 1917 as dictator of Russia, started this book in a group called the Social Revolutionaries, you probably wouldn't be surprised. But Lenin was actually part of the Social Democrat movement, whereas the Social Revolutionaries were an offshoot of the populists who wanted a rural revolution to give power, and land, to the peasants (they were hardcore terrorists who kept attracting socialists from other groups, like Bolsheviks, when they got bored of talking and wanted to blow something up). Even Marx began to think Russia's mass of peasants could satisfy his belief in economic revolutionary development. As for him, you can read many books about Marx the man, and Marxism the theory (which rather got out of control from what he intended), but we'll sum up the pseudo-scientific theory here: the control of economic production would be used by one class to exploit another, until that class was in a position to rise up and take control, and the same would happen to them. So in theory medieval feudalism (which we now say didn't exist) had the aristocracy ruling over serfs who worked the land. After the English Civil War and French Revolution a bourgeois class had taken over, using liberal ideas with capitalist use of money and private property, and as the industrial workers grew under this class they would rise, take power in a socialist revolution, and it was this that socialists expected (and capitalists feared) in Europe. There would then be a dictatorship of the proletariat, and a classless society would emerge, with no need for the state. For Marx, this was a scientific process you could see and would happen. You'll see in this book Russian socialists tackling the question of how Russia, still essentially medieval, could get to the socialist stage: with or without a liberal revolution?

Back to the Social Democrats. In 1898, Russian Marxists of different kinds had finally put aside differences and come together to form the Russian Social-Democratic Labour Party, and despite what the press might tell you, the 'democratic' part of that name wasn't outright hypocrisy at that point. The party was illegal in Russia, but they even managed to come together enough to hold a first congress—though only nine attendees at most made it and they were soon arrested. But thanks to a combination of growing anger at the world, the efficacy of Marxism's scientific veneer of Marxism, the oppression of Russian government and a fair amount of doing what was trendy, a second party congress was held in 1903. Lenin was in attendance.

41

Vladimir Ilyich Lenin was a professional revolutionary, which is a polite way of saying he talked a lot of violence but didn't do much work, and he had been taken from a life of legal study and reborn as a revolutionary by the execution of his brother by the Russian state (see the appendix for more detail). In the years leading up to the Second Party Congress he had become one of the leading members of the socialist debate, by co-founding party newspaper *Iskra* (*The Spark*), and writing the extremely influential polemic *What Is To Be Done?*

Lenin had argued with the other socialists before now. He had been involved in multiple debates, and had developed a bellicose style. He wanted centralization where other people wanted loose structures, although no one foresaw that this would become a dictatorship where dissident socialists would be arrested. He wanted strong personalities at the top, which basically meant him. He was afraid too many socialists wanted peaceful, almost liberal transition and evolution, where he wanted action, violent action, and people doing what they were told ... by him. It's a mistake to consider Marxism as one idea, because as soon as it left Marx's hands it became a myriad of variations. In Russia people tried to adapt Marx to a nation that was mostly rural, to the point where a very young Lenin blithely labelled Russia a capitalist nation ready for change, at which point literally everyone else he met pointed

42

out this was nonsense. Just as Marxists across Europe worked on how this theory fit their reality, the Marxists of Russia argued among themselves, about the role of middle classes, the role of liberals, how large a working class was needed and many other finer points. Lenin, after many non-starts and detours, came to the conclusion that the proletariat / working class would, if not given the right leadership, betray the Marxist inevitability of seizing production to settle into peace with the capitalists, and that a true revolution into a true communist state could only be achieved if this working class was led by a small group of dedicated intellectual revolutionaries. Or, as you're no doubt thinking, people like him, led by him. This was not what the other social democrats thought. He had taken the organization of the People's Will, bolted a perversion of Marxism at the bottom, and welded himself at the top. In lesser hands it might never have gained any traction. But for all the harm he did, and as this book will show, Lenin was a remarkable person who would turn this idea into control of a vast empire.

Wording Versus Personality

Technically the Bolsheviks emerged over a dispute at the second congress about the words used in article one of the party rules. Many, led by leading speaker Martov, wanted a loose structure which would include as many people as

43

possible, so allowed anyone who accepted the party's ideas (and would follow instructions) to be members of the party. This view was actually the majority among attendees. Lenin, however, wanted a much smaller hardcore of revolutionaries who were better ordered and controlled, people far more tightly bound to the party, actively taking part. It was a struggle between a smaller group of revolutionaries versus a broad-based movement of the whole people after democratic committees. And yet, it was a struggle about Lenin, because he wanted his way and his people and his party, and he didn't trust the mass of people to live up to the challenge.

A vote was held, and Martov's supporters won 28 to 23. However—and here we go—two smaller factions, numbering seven people, then walked out in disagreement with things, meaning Lenin's people came out ahead in the vote. This might not seem a problem—it was a vote over article one—but because Lenin and friends were now a majority, they became known as the Bolsheviks, the Majority, while Martov and friends became known as the Mensheviks, the Minority, even though the position was basically reversed. It set the tone for the publicity and grandstanding for years to come. Suddenly, Lenin could claim to be Bolshevik, the Majority, even though he rarely ever was. Someone had walked out, Lenin had gained an advantage. This will happen again, and it only gets worse for your average Russian as a result.

Bolshevik versus Menshevik

No one had any idea, of course, that this split would last. Socialist politics was like water running from a bath, the suds merged and split. But Lenin had been working on party newspaper *Iskra*, and wielded his position like an axe, expelling three of the Menshevik editors to make the paper Bolshevik (and in practice, Lenin's mouthpiece). The Mensheviks, led by Martov, were livid at this coup, at this dictatorship, but Lenin didn't seem to care. The groups stayed split. As time advanced, the Bolsheviks and Mensheviks formed sides, sometimes between people who joined the cult of Lenin and people who rejected it. In a sense, political differences only followed the very personal issue of whether you found Lenin inspirational or deranged. They were still all Social Democrats, and away from Lenin in rural Russia, SD groups went on ahead blissfully unaffected by the split. But now there were two opposed factions, one with a would-be leader determined everyone should follow him, one a loose group of dreamers who didn't want to.

That would-be is important, because the Bolsheviks didn't all obey Lenin slavishly at this point, they still argued and thought their opinions mattered. The Bolsheviks were still a Russian socialist party, and that means factional. But the divide was there, the start was happening: revolutionaries who turned to violence, under a violent leader, and another faction more democratic and willing to work with liberals and capitalists to push forward a different version of the communist end game. Many Mensheviks believed it necessary to turn Russia into a capitalist regime in order to then turn it into a socialist one, which might sound odd, but it's literally why so many worked with liberals in 1917. Lenin offered an immediate jump which appealed to a lot of discontent people, even if he was a dictator-like figure and the Mensheviks were more actual socialism.

Things Never Change

Lenin founded his own Bolshevik Party in 1912, although the fact he'd held his own Third Party Congress and not invited anyone Menshevik a few years before had basically already done this. In 1912 he found the Mensheviks rejecting him over part funding himself through robbery, a move which crippled his support, but he built it back up by portraying the Mensheviks as too safe, and attracting workers who wanted action now, a growth aided by the way he built on the Lena River massacre of protesting mine workers. Nevertheless, the events of 1917 were moulded by the characteristics of this early split. When 1917 arrived, the

46

Bolsheviks had a clearer message and a clearer leader than the hydra-headed and woolly Mensheviks, and this was true of them at the start and all the way through. But, and it's a massive but, while this is true, and is the clearest way of describing it, we must stress that Lenin had to argue and fight all the time to be followed. He did offer clear, stark leadership, but all Russian socialists were cats in need of herding, and in a sense what made Lenin successful was that he could, through extreme rhetoric and plain luck, do this. Bolshevik and Menshevik, the split and the victory, was about Lenin's violent personality more than people now like to admit. Even when the Mensheviks moved towards Lenin they could not reunite with him because they would have had to bow and scrape.

CRIB

- Socialism in Russia, and Europe, was divided into factions.
- Leader of one group, Lenin, wanted a small party of die-hard revolutionaries who did what he told them and would demand revolution soon.
- Another group formed, led by Martov, who wanted a broad party, with democratic decision making.

47

- The two fell out in a vote at the Second Party Congress but because people walked out, Lenin's minority group got more votes, and became known as Bolshevik (Majority). The actual largest became Mensheviks (Minority).

- The two sides never reconciled, and became increasingly opposed. One which Lenin led through force of personality, the other a cloud of (non) leadership.

4: Preconditions for Revolution (aka Context)

You don't need to read this chapter. If you wish to continue with the narrative of the Russian Revolution skip to the next section, because this is where we get the context. I hope this book explains the whys and whats well, but here we're going to look at fault lines of imperial Russia, the all-important background to why a nation was able to go through such a traumatic period. In short, we're tackling an essay question, but I'm always a fan of as much context as possible, which is why this book mentions Alexander II more than normal.

Russia in this period was a vast empire which reached from (not evenly remotely independent) Poland to the Pacific, included 165 million people, and a good many languages, religions and cultures.

The tsars might have wanted Russia to be a monolithic empire under them, but the reality was a pulsing, multi-faceted unit which pushed and pulled itself around. Ruling this state was always going to be difficult, but there were long-term fault lines eroding the Romanov monarchy which, in 1917, collapsed into a revolution which swept the old regime away. World War One was clearly the trigger event, but this chapter will look at the problems underpinning the rest of this narrative.

It's important to remember that no one marched into Russia and removed the Romanovs, not even the Kaiser's Germans, and the people at the bottom, the famed workers of hard left accounts, didn't come into play until after the Tsar had gone. The fall of Tsar Nicholas II came when the top of Russia collapsed. It's also important to note, in the timescale of this book, the final form of 1917 was not inevitable: revolution was averted in 1905, there were plenty of chances for reform. But the final tsars not only didn't want reform, they went backwards, all chance to save themselves was lost. At the start of 1917 something had to happen because almost everyone, from the military to the factory workers, wanted action, and the Tsar rejected the chance to have it be his actions, and his leadership which would retain his government.

Peasant Poverty

According to many a theorist before World War One, socialist revolutions had to have an industrial workforce, and the socialist groups you'll come across in this book spent plenty of time arguing about such ideas. Why? Just before the revolutions of 1917, three quarters of the entire Russian population were peasants who farmed in small villages. While I'm going to show that the start of 1917 didn't see a socialist

50

revolution, there had been one by the end and how they dealt
with peasants was important.

In theory, Russia's peasants were better off in 1916
than they had been in 1860, because before that they had been
serfs who were owned by landowners and who could be sold
like property. In 1861 the serfs were freed and given their own
holdings of land, and that sounds like a great idea until you
run into the government keeping control: in return for their
own land, the now freed serfs had to pay a sum back to the
government, resulting in a huge number of small farms deeply
in debt and still very much slaves to the people above them.

Russian agriculture was not romping ahead in the
development stakes, with the general condition of Russian
farms poor: no capital to invest, no education to learn about
improvements, techniques out of date as a result. Families
lived around subsistence level, and here's where some
socialism creeps in: half of all Russian farms had at least one
family member who had left the village to find work, and this
often meant the growing industrial towns. And yet, as the
Russian population rose, land in central Russia became scarce
and the elite forced debt ridden peasants to sell their land for
commercial use. A boon for the Russian agricultural industry,
a disaster for peasant life.

These peasants joined those travelling to the cities for
work. There they began to urbanise, and looked down on the

peasants they'd left behind even though the cities were like all the developing industrial centres: unplanned, overcrowded, dangerous, with poorly paid and extremely risky working conditions. At odds with their bosses and the elite, these workers formed a new class and a new urban culture, which was militant and prepared to take action. Ignoring the patronising liberals, these new workers preferred the socialists.

The rich landowners owned about a fifth of the land; they were also usually aristocrats. Western, more European farms, as well as the southern ones tended to have larger peasant farms with more commercialization. But, despite this, by 1917 Russia had a central mass of annoyed peasants who thought the government and the landowners were trying to control them and profiting from the land without working it. Sorry to generalise, but the average peasant mindset wanted more land, autonomy and no outside interference.

Strangely, despite the population of Russia being overwhelmingly either rural peasants or urban ex-peasants, the upper class of the country knew almost nothing of their real life but a load of myths: a noble, pure, almost holy communal existence. Yes, the peasants in these half a million villages were organized in mirs, the community leadership which followed centuries of practice and defined the legal, cultural and social nature of their lives (mir means commune, world and peace, and that tells you a lot about the peasant mindset).

52

However, these [Mirs] were not the happy, lawful communes of the elite's imagination, but a system of desperate struggle fed by humanity's flaws: theft, violence, elderly patriarchs. If you come from a capitalist and notionally democratic western country and want to know how the Bolsheviks were able to be so free with private property, look to the peasants. They had no private property: all family possessions were owned by the autocratic head of the household until he died, the sons divided it, and the households started again. Freed serfs weren't free in any western sense, and you can see quite clearly how the role of the Tsar was echoed in millions of peasants experience. The peasant class of Russia did not develop western political awareness, like a desire to keep private property, to vote, to have laws and courts. They developed a desire for strong action, including violence, out of their own moral imperative. It wasn't just communists who broke Russia apart in bloodshed.

During this period, a division was starting between the elders and a growing number of literate young peasants who wanted reform, but the mir was still a culture of deeply ingrained violence. The peasant view of the world was derived from custom, folk memory, and an abiding dislike of an interfering government. These insiders hated the outside. Soon we'll come to a man called Stolypin, and his land reforms which tried to break the family ownership of peasant land and turn it into capitalism. Frequently, in 1917, these peasants re-joined the communal systems. Peasants didn't see themselves as a class so much as the deliverers/ warriors for the justice of poor vs strong.

The elite landowners didn't have it all their own way. They might have had the ground, but when the serfs went so did their free labour. The elites had to find replacements and adapt to a capitalist world, and many couldn't. They started to fail, started to panic, and they too had to sell land. Some were like Prince Lvov, a man who will dominate the central part of this book, who became a zemstvo leader and made his farms run well, building schools, roads and more. But this was a problem too, because Tsar Alexander III was afraid the zemstvo committees were too liberal, and government laws attempted to dominate the zemstvos to the extent of sending out 'Land Captains' to enforce the Tsar's laws. In this way the counter reforms of the Romanovs smashed into the reformers and created a struggle over the land. Unhappy larger landowners, unhappy peasants, all unhappy with the Tsar as well as each other.

In 1917 the Tsar fell without reference to the land problems, but the liberal and socialist governments which followed ran straight into it: with the Tsar gone, peasants expected the elite landowners to redistribute wealth. The way the liberals and socialists treated this problem, or should we say totally ignored it until it was too late, doomed the February revolution and helped produce October. To generalise, most peasants weren't worried about constitutions and liberal democracy; they wanted a strong leader in the same way they wanted strong leadership from village elders, and they would view the end of the Tsar and the appearance of some wishy-washy liberals and socialists as the chance to use their own strong leadership to go after what they did want: the land of the wealthy.

I don't mean to cast the Russian peasants as brutes; I mean to show them as isolated, with no opportunity of education or citizenship, trapped in local prisons.

A Politicized and Urban Workforce

This section is what you might be expecting in a book on the Russian Revolution: it deals with a political group of workers. The industrial revolution really hit Russia in the 1890s (led, to their credit, by the Tsar and his government), bringing with it ironworks, factories and everything else the west had been experiencing as they industrialized. This development was neither as advanced nor as fast as in Britain, which basically led the way, but still produced large and rapidly growing cities filled with ex-peasants, leaving millions in dense, dirty urban areas. The government was afraid of this urban class because they knew the bad wages, bad conditions,

55

bad housing and lack of rights were making them angry. An 1897 law on working hours 'limited' the adult working day to eleven and a half hours. However, this government was more afraid of ruining foreign investment by reforming the treatment of these workers. One reason why the Tsar's government was so keen to stamp out strikes was its own leadership of industrialization.

You don't have to be a socialist to predict or understand what happened next: the workers turned their anger into a growing political culture, rejecting the government attacks on their protests, and looked to people who might have answers. And who did? The socialists, who found fertile soil for their activism. The government was so worried they actually created their own neutered trade unions to distract the banned but genuine and powerful real ones. In 1905 and 1917, politicized workers who had taken up a belief in socialism played major roles, but, and it's a massive but, 'socialism' was actually a hugely fragmented ideology with several powerful and competing factions. In many ways, the story of 1917 is a war between rival socialist thinkers.

There is another effect of industrialization. Much of the money to do this came in from abroad, a deliberate raising of foreign capital by a politician and economic champion called Witte, who put Russia on the gold standard. But with foreign money came a desire for peace, stability, western law-abiding actions and reforms. Industrialization might have made a workforce ripe for socialists, but it started an international squeeze.

You can argue a good point here. Russia was industrialising, with heavy government investment, and production was increasing and modernising. The Tsar and Witt were moving to bring Russia up to the industrial level of the west. However, they've been accused of industrialising 'too quickly', for while numbers soared up (like production figures) the stresses on society (such as rapid urbanization and terrible living conditions) increased too.

Autocratic Tsars Who Weren't Even Good At Autocracy

For three centuries Russia had been ruled by the Romanov family, who were a form of emperor known as tsars. The three hundredth anniversary actually occurred during the narrative of this book, 1913, and huge sums of money were spent on grand pageants. Romanov rule would survive for just four more years, but no one had any idea this would be the case, and every part of the festival was designed to ram home the natural right of the Romanovs to be in charge. The only people who listened to the propaganda were the royals themselves.

The tsars, which included female tsarinas like Catherine the Great, were autocrats: they ruled alone as the sole power in Russia, with no true representative bodies. The Duma, an elected body created in 1905 in the aftermath of a failed rebellion, doesn't count because it was completely ignored by the Tsar when he wanted to. Books and newspapers were censored, freedom of expression was low, and secret police operated to stop dissent, wielding executions and exile to Siberia. The tsars were, technically and in theory, the only people who could pass any law, and they could do so entirely at their whim.

It didn't matter whether you were democrat, revolutionary, republican, socialist or other, they all chaffed under the Russian regime and wanted reform. Some were driven by oppression to want violent change, others were peaceful, but as the Tsar shut down opposition, people became increasingly extreme. Russia was a very strict autocracy once Alexander II had died and Alexander III reacted with repression, a counter reform of centralized, authoritarian government.

A lot of this book covers the reign of Tsar Nicholas II, the man in charge in 1917 when it all went horribly wrong for his family (and, if we're being honest, for Russia too). He has been accused of weakness – his father certainly thought so and didn't bother to educate him – and of lacking the willpower needed to govern. Some historians, like Figes, argue this wasn't the case: they say Nicholas did have the will to govern, he was determined to do so, he just didn't have the required ability, or indeed any idea of how to run an autocracy properly. Nicholas's answer to the crises of the Russian regime, inherited from his much stronger father (a man who died before his son was remotely ready to take over), was to try and return Russia to a late-medieval, quasi-seventeenth century system instead of reform, triggering the massive discontent which led to revolution. On hearing of his father's death, Nicholas II said "I know nothing", referring to his new role as king, which is sad but shocking when you know that King Louis XVI, aka the one beheaded by the French Revolution, said basically the same thing. Both blamed their fathers for not teaching them how to rule.

Nicholas II had three core ideas he adhered to, based on the ideas of much earlier tsars: Russia was a fiefdom with a lord, namely him, and he owned it all; land ownership and power trickled down from him. Secondly, the Tsar had been given power by God, and couldn't be opposed by any earthly power. He ruled unrestrained. Thirdly, he was a tough but fair father to a Russian people who loved him. Not only did these views clash with the west and their emerging democracy, they clashed with many in Russia. That people 'strongly objected' to them doesn't go far enough. But the ideas of the west were coming east, eating into the foundations Nicholas was trying to bring back.

Of course, it was more complicated than this, because it always is: Russia didn't even have just one kind of autocracy. Peter the Great's vision was western, and organized royal power in a system of laws and bureaucracies that still remained as 'Petrine Autocracy'. But Alexander III, heir of the murdered, reforming Alexander II, had reacted and tried to send Russia back to a tsar-centric, personalized, 'Muscovite Autocracy'. The two existed together and warred. Petrine followers had become interested in reform, in listening to people, and consequently a constitution. Nicholas II was also Muscovite, and wanted pretty much the opposite. Even a dress code was present in Nicholas II's old order.

The Tsar had some old help: the idea of the good tsar, who protected you, with the evil coming from the boyars, aristocrats and other landowners. Unfortunately for the Romanovs, fewer people in the twentieth century believed it. Alexander III was a strong personality who could force things to happen. He died in 1894, aged forty-nine. Nicholas wasn't interested in politics, had little idea about the nature of Russia, had little education in running a nation or government, and had a weak personality. He didn't trust other people, couldn't delegate, and was desperate to keep all power to himself. He wasn't a good ruler for an autocracy, and would have been

60

great in Britain where he could have paraded round and let a parliament do everything. But he wasn't in Britain.

The men who tried to reform Russia, who could see what was happening, able men like Stolypin, had to deal with a tsar who openly resented them, who wouldn't disagree to people's faces but would change his mind later, who would only see ministers individually so a group wouldn't overwhelm him. The Russian system was flawed and weak, but it was made worse because government couldn't work as the Tsar didn't delegate or appoint able officials. Nicholas II sat in charge of a vacuum that could not react to changing and revolutionary currents.

There was a tsarina of course, Nicholas's wife. She is considered to be the stronger personality, who wasn't afraid to offend people and often did, who felt her husband did not need to be liked to be strong, and who could direct him. She worked hard to strengthen Nicholas's backbone, but despite coming from a European family, bought massively into the Russian autocratic dream, and her strengthening was designed to stop the Tsar making any concessions at all, neither for him, or for her son, both of whom she regarded as children. However, as she struggled with this haemophiliac boy she drifted ever further into mysticisms which, as we'll see, damaged the royal family further, especially when dealing with con-man mystic Rasputin.

Bad Government

The elites at the top of Russian society were mostly aristocratic landowners, but some of the civil service had achieved their position without land. Either way, these elites ran the state and the bureaucracy and were a class above the general population. However, whereas some countries had developed elites who acted as a counter to the ruler, in Russia the landed and the elite depended on the Tsar. Indeed, Russia had a strict set of civil service ranks that decided your job, your uniform, and where you advanced automatically once you were in. This didn't mean Russia had a strong system, just an antiquated one that was falling apart, a weak and failing government that lacked, and was losing, the skills and people to govern. The civil service was essentially a body of tsarist servants. You swore service to the tsar when you joined and you couldn't quit unless he gave you permission, which led to some awkward moments. Russia's government was an overlapping chaos, full of jealous rivalry, division and rule from the Tsar, confusion and greed, with laws smashing into other laws and the Tsar able, should he wish, to overrule it all. It looked archaic and idiotic, unfair and autocratic, because it was. The bureaucracy had been prevented from becoming modern, efficient or professional, let alone a counter to a quasi-medieval monarch. There was an immunity from

62

prosecution too, because you could only be tried if your boss agreed, and they usually didn't want to risk blame.

This chaos wasn't an accident, it was the result of policy. In the aftermath of the Crimean War, professional civil servants led an attempt to reform and strengthen the state on the western model so all future wars would be won, and this included the great reforms of the 1860s, like freeing the serfs (although, as we've seen, they only sort of did that). In 1864 this led to the creation of the zemstvo's as local assemblies which created a level of self-rule. The 1860s were years of liberal hope and progressive reform which led to the west. The reforms were costly and difficult and needed years, but they were there.

There were opponents, but not all the Russian elites were with them—in fact they were divided. The reformists of Russia accepted calls for political freedoms, equal laws, aid for the working class and acceptance of the middle. They called for a constitution, and Alexander II considered a modest one. But there were rivals who wanted the old order, and many of these were in the military. They wanted autocracy, the nobility, church and, naturally, the military as the cornerstones of rule. The start of the Russian tragedy was the death of Alexander II. His 1860s meant people had tasted reform, lost it … and many looked for revolution.

There were eighty-nine provincial capitals, but imperial government evaporated below that. Russia didn't have the money or the foundations to support anything deeper. Peasants ran things their own way, methods alien to an elite who didn't understand them. Local areas were, by standards of both the west and anyone who wanted anything done, under-governed, and as the old regime was not all-powerful or all-seeing (as some of them wanted), government was absent and out of touch. A small number of police, who were state officials, were increasingly co-opted by the state for pretty much any task as there wasn't anyone else, and I mean checking-the-state-of-the-roads any task. The tax system was small with no one willing to expand it, communications were bad and the serfdom had ended with landowners still in charge. The Tsar's government was not meeting the civilians and discontent was growing.

The zemstvos became key, as the landowning nobles, with no state reaching down to them and in decline, used these small committees to fight against industrialization and all the other problems of agriculture in this era. Until the revolution of 1905 the zemstvos were a liberal movement, asking for more local power, a constitution at the top, a representative parliament and help in the battle of peasant versus landowner. It was the zemstvo nobility who would provide the early revolution in 1917, not the workers.

64

Disaffected Military

In theory, the military was the biggest supporter of the Tsar, but it was also riven with tension. Perhaps the most obvious cause of this was that the country kept losing wars, including Crimea, Turkey and as we have just seen, Japan, and the military decided to blame this on the government rather than themselves. They had an easy target, as military expenditure had declined. Russian industrialization wasn't as advanced as the west, so Russia lagged behind, badly trained, badly equipped and with a long losing streak. Soldiers, and the more conscious officers, were demoralized. It's useful to note here that soldiers were at this point sworn to serve the Tsar, not the Russian state. Many dreaming, deluded officers preferred to worry about button details rather than fix their feudal army.

There was another reason the army was fracturing, and why morale was low. More and more the troops were being used by provincial governors in stopping peasant revolts. As most of the troops were peasants themselves, you can see why this was causing problems. Indeed, these peasants were treated by officers as serfs, as sub-civilian slaves, and in 1917, when revolution began, the soldiers joined in, demanding reform of the military as much as the rest of the country.

I mustn't paint the officer class as too foolish. There was a growing group of professional military people who saw what the west was doing, saw the flaws in the system – from weapon supply to trench tactics – and demanded reforms of this. For these men the Tsar and the government were stopping the military from working, and they increasingly turned to the Duma (which we will meet after 1905) as an outlet. The most talented military men in the country were turning away from the Tsar.

The Church

Russia was the Orthodox Church, and the Orthodox Church was Russia. The people had a foundation myth about defending, even being at one with, this branch of Christianity. The west didn't have anyone like the politico-religious figure that the Tsar was in Russia, and he or she could wield the church to destroy people as much as they could use laws (a lot). The state found the church vital for controlling mostly illiterate peasants, and priests not only preached obedience to the Tsar, but reported infractions to the police. When Alexander III and Nicholas II looked backward, the church went willingly.

However, the church had a problem. Industrialization was moving millions of peasants into secular cities, where the church lagged behind. This was a problem of all churches in industrialising nations, but the Orthodox church did not adapt to urban life, or the reforms being called for by liberal clergy, who knew that such changes were only possible with a move away from these new tsars. The church found its message ignored, because socialism better answered the needs of the workers, not their version of Christianity. Peasants could also be sceptical of the church, disliking them as tools of outside control and preferring something positively pagan.

Politicized Civil Society

As we saw in chapter one, Russia had developed a political culture. These educated professionals were not large enough to be a true middle class, but they were emerging between the upper class and the peasants and workers. This was a 'civil society' whose youth became students, who engaged in debates and read newspapers, who served the public good rather than the Tsar. They were largely liberal, and if you skipped chapter one, a terrible famine in 1891 had shown them how ineffective the Tsar's government was, and how effective their own response had been, so why not let them unite and work? The zemstvo led the way. The Tsar refused to meet the new political class anywhere near halfway, and they began to radicalise.

Nationalism

Russia was an empire built from many different regions and old states, and when modern nationalism came into this world neither the Tsar, the liberals, nor any branch of government could deal with it. Campaigns to break away from the empire, for independence, began to grow and destabilise regions, and it was the socialists who grasped nationalism and promoted regional independence. Socialist nationalists were actually the most effective type of nationalist. Of course, this was humanity so there were many shades of grey, and some nationalists wanted to remain in the mother empire and simply gain more power. Naturally, the Tsar made it all worse by not just repressing nationalism but pushing Russifying campaigns, transforming cultural movements into snarling political-national opposition. Tsars had always Russified, but this was even more divisive.

Repression and Revolution

In 1825, the uprising of the Decembrists started a counter attack that included the formation of a prototype police state (under, of all people, Nicholas I, namesake of 1917's failure). Censorship was mixed with a system of investigators called the Third Section. In 1881, under the counter reforms, this became the Okhrana, a fully-fledged secret police who embedded agents everywhere fighting a shadow war against transgressives, a war that included having agents pretend to be revolutionaries. They could punish people with exile to Siberia for just being suspected of acts and thoughts against the state without any proof, and if they did have proof you could be tried under wartime military law. The police gave you permission when it came to jobs or social events, they answered to no lawyers or judiciary, they were a repressive force in a country that didn't have that many actual revolutionaries, just a genuinely disaffected population. The Bolshevik and Stalinist police states started here, under the tsars.

Revolutionaries were locked in Tsarist prisons and exiled to Siberia, but this didn't exactly stop rebellion. Rather, the system pushed the weak away and hardened the rest into extremists who started as Russia's intellectuals, readers and thinkers, and transformed them into cold, violent men and women. They were derived from the Decembrists of the 1920s and built a succession of generations of revolutionaries who inspired the next, always evolving. Rejected and attacked by the government, hated by the Tsar, many turned from peace to violence and dreams of a glorious battle. Any study of twenty-first century terrorism finds the same thing world over, the pattern is clear, the warning was there. Of course it wasn't just revolutionaries: the Tsarist repression pushed believers in all sorts of politics together, because almost all sorts were banned, and then radicalized them to the point where even

69

liberals wanted the Tsar gone. When all political opposition had to be done in secret, it was easy to develop a conspiratorial outlook, and the literature of Russian opposition began to promote strong, hard, emotionless characters who would take difficult, deadly decisions.

Some experts have concluded that western reforming ideas were transformed when they reached Russia, because censorship suppressed them and turned them into strongly believed dogma, able to drive people to violence. Many famous revolutionaries were normally from a class above the working people, looked to them as a rose-tinted ideal, and used the state as an opposite, hating it with guilt-inspired anger. These intellectuals had no real idea about peasants, just a fantasy, an abstraction that twisted people to authoritarianism.

The idea of a small group of socialist revolutionaries taking power and creating a dictatorship to both install a socialist society and remove enemies was not new in 1917—in fact the golden age was the 1860s. But by 1917 these ideas had sometimes turned dark and brutal, based on hate. This period didn't have to end in Marxism, as initially many revolutionaries chose other socialisms, but something remarkable happened to Marx and his book *Capital*: the Russian censor cleared it for publication in Russia because they believed it to be too impossible to understand to be a threat, relating to an industrial world Russia didn't have. The story of socialism in Russia is one of petty jealousy and farce, and Marx's involvement began the same way: not only was the censor awfully wrong, *Capital* was a massive hit, the trend of the day. The intellectuals and revolutionaries had seen one movement fail, so Marx was the new one, the hipster beard of the late nineteenth century. No more populism, no need to go near strange peasants, but the closer world of workers. Marx seemed to be logic and science and a new world, modern, not dogma.

Lenin stands as an example of how Russia made a revolutionary. He was training to be a lawyer when his older brother was executed for terrorism. Rather than being put off, he went into rebellion, and was expelled from university, so looked to previous Russian revolutionary groups and became one himself. Only then, already a rebel, did he find Marxism, which he rewrote to fit Russia.

Lenin at first followed the ideas of Russian Marxist leader Plekhanov, and recruited urban workers via strikes for improved rights. There were 'legal Marxists' who wanted a peaceful transition but Lenin, born from death, committed to forceful revolution, and a counter party to the Tsar, organized strictly. They created the newspaper *Iskar* (*The Spark*) to recruit and order their members, and Lenin was part of the Social Democratic Party.

In 1902 he wrote *What Is To Be Done?*, a violent work which explained his vision. It's at this point something happened which seems almost silly, and that's how the Social Democrats divided into two groups, the Bolsheviks and Mensheviks, at the second Party Congress in 1903. This is discussed in more detail in chapter three, but essentially Lenin's dictatorial views caused it, as he was a centraliser who trusted only himself, an anti-democrat, and the process was quite frankly ridiculous.

Tectonic Plates Grinding

These pre-conditions weren't just lying in wait in Russia, they were like great tectonic plates grinding against each other, building to an earthquake. You had a vast body of Russian peasants, rural and insulated, with an often western looking nobility and government above them, and a cramped, industrial workforce alongside them, all three rubbing along in distrust. Russia was producing some of Europe's most accomplished culture, but masses of peasants were illiterate. Russia had great natural resources but lagged behind western powers and began to feel insecure. Furthermore, Russians in Russia made up only a minority of the grand Russian Empire, and as the new nationalism spread to these peripheral lands, further tensions were stirred up. Russia was a mass of rivalry and contradiction.

World War One

The trigger for revolution in 1905 and 1917 was war, or, more accurately, doing badly in war. In 1905 the failures of the Russian government helped trigger the opposition, but when the same Tsar went to war in 1914 he was firing the starting gun on the collapse of his empire. The three years of the Great War stressed and convulsed Russia to the point that the Tsar was rejected by enough key people to drive him out and begin a year of revolutions. This will be explained in more exasperating, farcical detail later in the book. For now, we return to 1905.

CRIB

- Most of the Russian population were peasants, and most lived in backward communities led by centuries of folk tradition. They were angry at not having enough land and being in debt, and demanded land 'reform' (taking it from the rich). The rich weren't much happier.

- A growing industrial and urban workforce lived in hellish conditions, and found socialism a natural belief to follow to solve their many problems and demands. The Tsar certainly wasn't listening to them.

- Russia was ruled by the autocratic Romanov family, and by Nicholas II, a man who hated reform and was determined to go back to something quasi-medieval. He believed he alone was the power in Russia. He just wasn't very good at wielding this power.

- Government in Russia included a muddled, competing, aristocratic top level with almost no link to the local units below them. It was inefficient in the extreme, and obeyed the Tsar at the top and disliked him at the bottom.

- The military was disaffected, annoyed at losing, annoyed at the Tsar for not reforming, angry at officers for treating them badly, and any combination of the three. Soldiers were also growing angry at having to put down revolts from brother peasants.

- The church found itself increasingly ignored by urban workers.

- A class of politically aware and active Russians was growing.

- Nationalism was pulling at the fringes of this massive, polyglot Russian empire. The Tsar's reaction was repression and Russification.

- The repression and secret police of the Tsarist state had helped produce a class of revolutionaries, while many angry and disaffected Russians had turned to a new theory that seemed to offer hope: Marxism, a seductive, pseudo-scientific idea.

- The Stalinist horror state originated and grew out of later Tsarist Russian policy.

- Wars caused change, and Russia kept losing their conflicts.

5: The Failed Revolution of 1905

Bloody Sunday

The revolution of 1905 had grown out of years of frustration with the Tsar, and the failed war against Japan had brought everything into focus. But the trigger was a workers' march. On January 9th, 1905, in a snow-covered St. Petersburg, Father Gapon led a march which would swell to 150,000 people towards the Winter Palace to deliver a demand for better working conditions. The government knew this march was coming, and twelve thousand soldiers were on duty to stop any 'problems', which basically meant preventing workers getting too close, too upset or even too keen. The stage was set for an explosion, as fatalistic workers who knew they were in danger marched towards lines of armed military. And yet, this is the Russian Revolution, so you know something patently bizarre was happening, and here it is: Father Gapon was leading a government-invented group.

In the years before the march, S. Zubatov came up with a cunning plan. He had been a Populist terrorist before he joined the Okhrana (the secret police aimed at stopping such people), and he knew that there were many, many discontent people in Russia. He also believed that if nothing was done these people would turn to revolutionary groups like socialists. His answer was a pragmatic piece of divide and rule: why didn't the state create their own unions and other labour organizations, to promote the idea of the Tsar as a stern but fair father figure who looked after his workers, and use these allied unions to pull people away from the socialists? Zubatov received backing and set some up, and although they began to unravel and he lost support and was fired because even this was too much, Gapon had been an ally, and the priest had his own workers and church group which was meant to make people stick with the Tsar.

However, the group radicalized. Desperate workers joined it and started pushing for help. They produced a programme of reform which included eight-hour working days (plausible for us) and a government that listened to people (rather ambitious given the circumstances). Gapon himself was also exceeding his remit, having become the sort of priest who thinks he was sent by God, and who thought the Tsar was a good, God-given man who would help if someone, namely Gapon, acted as a middle man between the ruler and the workers. The workers told Gapon what they wanted, Gapon told the workers it would happen.

When workers went on strike in early January 1905, Gapon thought his moment had come and organized a mass procession with a presentation-cum-petition to be delivered to the Tsar. This wasn't a secret, and the government tried to ban it, by which I mean they banned it, but the workers and Gapon were going to go ahead anyway: the former because some felt it was worth the risk, some felt the Tsar would help, some because they thought soldiers wouldn't fire on the crowd, and Gapon because he was in his own world. His oratory propelled forward tens of thousands of people, men, women and children, banners flying.

On this occasion, in 1905, they were twelve years too early, and as the columns of marchers closed in on the lines of soldiers, the latter fired into the air, and then into the crowd. What happened next was panic for both marcher and soldier, as the latter kept shooting and all hell broke loose. I'm not using that as a cliché, I'm saying it because Gapon was heard to say there is no God. All over the city, marcher met soldier and the killing started. It wasn't just troops with guns; there was also cavalry with swords were charging about. Some had hope still, and at the Nevsky Prospect a crowd of tens of thousands formed opposite soldiers who had artillery with them. Here too the army fired, this time using cannon, and among the fatalities could be seen children. The damage wasn't just physical, torn limbs, but mental: to the people of St. Petersburg, the good Tsar had been proved a myth. The real Tsar was firing into them and killing them en masse. The crowd divided, some fleeing for their homes, some turning into the sort of violent, thieving, vandalising mob that we see in riots across the world, this time driven on by the anger of a massacre.

Gapon was alive, and before he ran to Finland, issued an appeal for workers to rise and crush the Tsar; there is no anger quite like the disillusioned fanatic. The mob violence had no leaders to turn it into a movement, the violence dissipated and it stopped. Hundreds had been killed, more wounded.

The Russian Revolution: Take 1

On hearing about Bloody Sunday, or even having been in it, the mood of St. Petersburg was thick with anger and many felt a revolution had started. They might not want it, although some demanded it as recompense, but it felt like something had changed. Certainly, masses of workers came out to strike in the days and weeks that followed, hundreds of thousands of protestors in the largest wave of industrial action Russia had ever seen. But there were no leaders for these workers yet, as the socialists' revolutionary command, including Lenin and Trotsky, were all abroad in their exile, and not exactly rushing back just in case this was all a mistake. The terrorists were still around and they ramped up their actions, even killing Grand Duke Sergei, who was both Governor-General of Moscow and an uncle of the Tsar.

The people on the ground in Russia were lower ranking socialists, and students were so vigorous that practically every university was temporarily shut. The big names and leaders who were acting loudly were the liberals. They were outraged, and liberal outrage was a bit different then. Nowadays it's rants on Twitter but back then they used their zemstvos to agitate for an entire constituent assembly to build a new constitution. The Second National Congress of Zemstvos was held in April, when the anger and strikes were enough to keep propelling it. Liberals, professionals, democrats, they all started banding together in their own unions and demanding reform. It wasn't socialist rhetoric, but slogans such as 'we can't live like this'. And yet, how else could they achieve that change in the autocratic, repressive Russian system without being drawn to revolution, without feeling closer to the worker who wants massive structural change through physical, maybe violent action?

It's worth stressing that now, and from every point on in this book: when I talk about Russia experiencing strikes and unrest, in the lands of the empire where a growing national identity and nationalism looked to a non-Russian past and future (like Poland), everything was coloured and affected by this nationalism. Liberals and socialists argued and fought for reform, but often more autonomy if not independence.

Rural peasants also reacted to Bloody Sunday and the ongoing unrest, but not to support the workers. Instead, they started by going after what they thought was morally theirs but held by the rich, like wood and pasture, and then went after their possessions and their large houses. The countryside had a mob too, many of them, and they acted out of either jealousy over wealth or a desire for recompense depending on whether it was your house they were storming. Yet, they also created their own unions and communes, and even their own peasant republics, where the collapse of government rule (as the latter were busy with the cities) was replaced by peasant-run nations. Actual peasant presidents, running massively progressive agendas like getting universal suffrage and education. They were all crushed in the end, but while the soldiers were used elsewhere, these were a tremendous experiment.

Speaking of soldiers, we now come to the key difference between 1905 and 1917. The army was being used to stop worker and peasant rebellions, and the army was made up of workers and peasants, so they began to fray at having to fight. But, and it's a big but, in 1905 they mostly stayed in support of the Tsar, and did act to put down revolt.

Mostly, because 1905 gave the world two pregnant words: Potemkin and Odessa. The former was a Russian battleship in the Black Sea Fleet where a complaint over awful conditions turned into an execution and a mutiny, and the crew sailed to Odessa. Here, they staged a piece of powerful theatre, as the striking workforce, who had paralysed the city for several weeks, now paraded to mourn the body of slain crew. However, they were massacred by troops costing over 2000 lives, and forced to flee to Romania. As far as giant signs to the world that something was wrong go, you can't script much better.

The Tsar Acts Uselessly, and the Soviet Forms

The government reacted. It had to do something. However, it didn't react very fast because Nicholas II didn't realise there was a revolution. He once famously scolded a government minister by asking if the man was afraid a revolution would start. He had to be told politely, and very carefully, it already had.

Firstly, Russia couldn't fight the war with Japan, they needed their troops, so that was ended.

Secondly, an imperial decree acknowledged faults with the government, invited people to send in their complaints and said a national assembly would be pondered on. The aim was to blame the government, not the Tsar, make him the positive figure who would help, and then delay acting until everyone had calmed down and gone home. The people of Russia accepted this, flooding him with letters from schools, factories, villages, all explaining the problems. What did they want? A proper parliament. What did Nicholas's ministers produce after ignoring the people? A glorified echo chamber, a body designed solely for consultation drawn from a very narrow electorate. It was a Duma, and it was tightly controlled. The main aim was solely to stop Nicholas II going the way of the Grand Duke (and Alexander II).

The people were not satisfied, which is to say they reacted in two ways. Zemstvo leaders got together and drew up a draft constitution, which was advanced but achieved nothing, while the workers reacted in September and October by holding the first general strike in Russian history, to really make clear they were not happy, and not going to go away. The strikers, the workers, the peasants: as time wore on they were being radicalized, not just because socialist revolutionaries were arriving to take charge (although they were), but because weeks of tension and the verge of open war were transforming them. The difference between criminals and people in love with violence, and people showing opposition to those above them, broke down, as did peace. Russia became more violent overall.

I've mentioned St. Petersburg a lot, but the general strike started in Moscow, when printers striked. Then it spread across the whole country, not because any one leader ordered it, but because union after union, factory after factory, joined in. Russia was utterly paralysed and sliding into anarchy. They were demanding a constitutional assembly.

In St. Petersburg, something happened that would colour the next century of world history. On October 17th, 1905, over five hundred metalworkers gathered in the Free Economic Society building, pushed on by Menshevik activism, and elected a council of fifty members, including Bolsheviks, Mensheviks and Social Revolutionaries (hereafter SRs), to represent them and take executive action, and form a new workers' government to rival the old one. They called it a soviet. It organized food, strikes, a defence militia, had a newspaper, and inspired soviets in the other cities of Russia. Naturally, given that they ended up running this show, Lenin (who only arrived in November) and his Bolsheviks didn't have much control of it (Mensheviks did) and they didn't really like it existing. If there was one single driving force, it was the Menshevik Trotsky, one of the few revolutionaries who did rush back, and he was in practical charge.

The Tsar is Persuaded to Act Competently

You might be thinking that Nicholas II was very worried, given we've just rushed through nearly a year of strikes. He wasn't, he was mostly out obliviously hunting, until Witte finally got through to him with the binary demand: either stay as you are by calling in the whole army to stop this, or change things and reform. Witte then did what useful employees always do, which is produce a solution after demanding action: he had a document outlining civil liberty, a constitution, a working cabinet, a democratic Duma. Plenty of people backed Witte up, and the latter was being clever, because he aimed to meet the demands of the liberals, split them from the socialists, and bring peace through division, albeit with reform. Nicholas listened, and still asked his uncle, Grand Duke Nikolai, to wield the troops like a bludgeon and become dictator.

I'd like to say the Grand Duke was sensible and refused, instead asking for Nicholas to reform, but what actually happened was the borderline loony Grand Duke Nikolai threatened to shoot himself on the spot if Nicholas didn't reform. So yes, the problems in Russia really did start at the top. Hating himself for doing it but seeing no other option, Nicholas conceded some reform. He was humiliated in his own mind, and deserves no credit, as he planned to back-peddle as soon as the opportunity arose.

Witte's *October Manifesto* was published, and people celebrated. To the liberals, it looked like they had won. To the left-wing workers, people had not died in vain. Revolutionaries were not happy at being undercut, but the result was a success: the general strike was called off, and people began to enjoy new political freedoms like the right to be members of a political party.

Russia was about to get a new culture.

The Kadets

We've met several of the socialist parties acting in Russia, and certainly the important ones for this story: the SRs, and the two types of SDs, Menshevik and Bolshevik. Now it's time for you to meet a liberal party, as the main one formed in this period. They were the Constitutional Democrats, although then as now they were better known as the Kadets. It was the party of the zemstvo leaders and representatives, and it took their old programme (a national zemstvo assembly) and built on it to demand universal voting rights, civil rights, nods to nationalism and more. It housed the middle ground, the middle class, and was soon a hundred thousand strong. Many were lower ranking nobles, some were high ranking nobles, few were industrial workers. University professors dominated, and that was reflective of the character of the party: these were not politicians, skilled in getting things done. They were talkers and thinkers and self-proclaimed leaders of the masses who had no mandate beyond their own ego. Don't read this description and think the Kadets were united: like every party, they were fiercely divided over many issues, with a large left and right wing. They were

86

joined by zemstvo hero Prince Lvov, a man who typified their character and who became a bridge for left and right. We will meet him in more detail in 1917.

The Kadets were thus demanding major reforms, and not loyally following the Tsar. Liberals who wished to do that could join the Octobrist Party, whose aim was to live by the October Manifesto and nothing more. They were liberal monarchists. Both types of liberals now had a chance to work with the Tsar, as leading members were invited to form the new cabinet-style government.

But were they? Okay, leading liberals were offered jobs by Witte in the new government, but there was a reason why the liberals refused to take them. On questioning, Witte could not guarantee the Tsar would follow the October Manifesto through, and the liberals found they had a choice: they had been leading this 1905 revolution. Did they now move towards support of the Tsar and trust him, and risk losing the workers, or did they stay in opposition, keep the workers, and demand real, structurally massive change? The Tsar and Witte, although mostly Witte, had been clever, and had started to divide the liberals from the socialists and split up what had been a mass rebellion into smaller, manageable blocks. The question was: did the liberals do what they could with this government?

They've been accused ever since they demurred at this point of throwing away their chance to reform the system from the inside, but that does rather require a belief the Tsar would ever have changed. This writer tends to think he wouldn't. Indeed, he was more interested in the right-wing groups, because the extreme monarchists (and, as we shall see, racists) were forming their own parties.

The Black Hundreds

The main right-wing party was the Union of the Russian People, whose aim was to fight the left, and did so by openly hating liberals, socialists and Jews. They formed bands of street fighters called Black Hundreds who marched, attacked and ravaged the opposition, and who were supported by a monarchy and government whose Tsar wore their symbol. Stop me if you've heard this before, because yes, this was a proto-Nazi movement. Anyone who felt threatened by reform, other people or economic changes all flocked to this wing. They murdered thousands, and the right-wing police ignored it, while the government funded it. Witte, trying to make things work, protested and was ignored.

Where Were The Bolsheviks?

As Russia experienced a revolution, the socialist leaders were doing what they did best, which was petty infighting. Lenin held his own Social Democrat Party congress, to which he only invited Bolsheviks, and elected a central committee composed just of those. The Mensheviks followed by doing the same. In Russia, people were dying. In London and Geneva they were acting like children.

However, as Russia sat on the precipice, Lenin returned and his Bolshevik party was plotting an armed uprising. But this was Lenin, a man at this point living half in a world of violent fantasy, and he knew they couldn't actually seize power as he had too little support, he just wanted to make the gesture (in 1917 he would be far more careful). December 3rd was the day the Tsar arrested the St. Petersburg Soviet, and the day the Moscow Social Democrats rose. Within days they had seized key parts of the city, but the Tsar still had the rest of Russia, and he still had the army, and this arrived and crushed the rebellion. State murder and torture followed as the counterrevolution was launched, not just in Moscow, but across Russia. Thousands were executed, tens of thousands locked up, and people fled abroad again, all with the sight of the Duma in the future. 1905 was over.

Why Did The Revolution Fail?

The most obvious reason why 1905 ended with the Tsar still in power and a Duma forming was that the military stayed mostly loyal to the Tsar. This would be very different in 1917, when three years of world war had severed the bonds of monarchy and military which stayed intact here. There were lots of mutinies and rebellions among the military in 1905, but not a tipping point.

There are also structural reasons, because the revolutionaries and rebellions from across this year had little overall leadership, with the revolution was over by the time the Duma opened, with the socialists led by grassroots support who localized and did not gain any overall momentum. This too, would change in 1917, when the Duma already existed to take a lead and a Soviet would form faster to bring so much of the left together (and while both would fail quickly, they had already done the job of removing the Tsar).

Furthermore, Witte's attempt to divide the rebellious had been perfect, and the opposition in 1905 had divided to the point where the socialist leaders could be hammered as the liberals signed up for talking shops.

Consequences of 1905

But this book didn't start in 1917, and some key changes had been wrought. Firstly, 1905 threw off shackles of repression, giving Russia a political culture which allowed Kadets, Octobrists and socialists who hadn't yet got arrested to form and speak. Censorship was relaxed, a Duma existed. 1905 saw Russia change, not as much as the rebellious had wanted, but in key ways. That the Duma would be a total failure leads us to 1917, but for now it gave Russia a new, unknown dimension. Mentality also changed. Never mind that people had the right to meet in a room. For many, the ancient and fabled vision of the Tsar as the tough but kind paternal figure, as the hope of the people against the grasping aristocrats, as good, had been shattered, broken in the minds of socialists and liberals alike.

But what replaced it? The liberals had their Duma and a chance to work with it, and would become disillusioned to that over time. For everyone else, they were not only annoyed with their Tsar, they had to return to their old factories and farms, and saw the liberals cheering, and realized that if they wanted reform it would not come from the liberals at all. In a very real sense, when the Tsar divided the liberals and socialists, he ensured the latter lost faith in the former and would look to their own socialist leaders for support.

And what leaders. Trotsky had been arrested and put on trial with a group of fellow socialists leaders. What normally happens when a failing regime gives a charismatic rebel a chance to grandstand in court happened, and Trotsky put on a display that converted and thrilled. Most went free, and Trotsky was just exiled, point well made. To your worker, and your peasant, the Trotskys of this world were the people to support, as 1905 and liberals had failed them.

91

Landowners and factory workers who had survived looked at their labour with a renewed desire to react against them. They grew more conservative. The liberals, Kadets included, shared this growing horror, this feeling that a revolution from below would unleash pent-up violence and sweep them away too. They began to fear the people, not want to lead them. They wanted change, but not extreme change. Russia was dividing, and this would affect what happened in the next twelve years.

The SD split crystallized, and Lenin – always a ponderer – came to the conclusions that would colour the rest of his revolutionary career: peasants could effect a socialist revolution, they did not need to wait for capitalism; the liberals and middle class were useless, and could be removed with the Tsar; and the nationalists were a ripe source of revolutionaries. The workers, the peasants, the Poles and others, all could form a revolutionary government after a violent overthrow of the rest. This approach, taken back into Russia by agents, would see the Bolsheviks, who had been nearly wiped out by counterrevolution, grow in support. The Mensheviks still thought they needed to work with liberals, and support revolutions elsewhere, in industrial Europe.

CRIB

- The Russo-Japanese War of 1905 embarrassed the Tsar.

- A march in St. Petersburg to deliver a petition was fired on by troops and a massacre followed.

- Russia rised in rebellion, with peasants and workers alike marching, striking and rioting.

- Liberals pushed for a constitution. A 'soviet' of workers formed to promote revolution.

- The Tsar was prodded down the road to compromise, and while early attempts and suggestions failed, Witte and others persuaded the Tsar to issue the October Manifesto.

- The revolution was broken as the opposition was divided by the Manifesto, and the promise of an elected Duma parliament.

- The liberals formed into political parties: the Kadets and the Octobrists.

- The right wing formed into proto-fascist groups like the Black Hundreds.

- The Tsar survived because the army stayed mostly loyal and there was no major opposition leadership.

- 1905 affected 1917 because it created the Duma and the Soviet, major players in the big revolution, and ended the myth of Tsarist power and competence.

6: Misfires at Change

The First Duma

I said the revolution of 1905 failed, yet it produced the Duma. Well, this is why. The Duma of the October Manifesto, the great hope of liberal Russia, opened on April 27th, 1906. To fill it the deputies travelled to see the Tsar in the Winter Palace. That's a simple sentence, fourteen words, but one filled with symbolism, because the Duma was to meet and barely function in the Tauride Palace. For this opening the Tsar made them come to his world, stand in his palace, see him on a throne in the coronation hall. The event was pure theatre of the sort that still works today: the Tsar, the aristocracy, the government all had uniforms. The Duma members turned up in their dark suits, and these two sides regarded each other. All you needed was a few workers still dirty from their factories and some peasants carrying hay and you'd have the three estates. (In fact, there were peasant deputies, and they established a reputation for hard drinking, with one member infamously turning up to speak bandaged from a pub brawl the night before. Duma immunity soon proved not to extend to fists in alehouses.)

The next eleven years were essentially a struggle between the Duma / the parliament, and the crown / the monarchists. Both thought the other was wrong, and wanted different government. The latter very much had the advantage, as while the October Manifesto seemed to give ground to reform, the Tsar didn't think much of it and didn't want to follow through. He wanted the Manifesto and any new to temper the rest of Russia, not him. He didn't call the constitution a constitution, he called it Fundamental Laws, as if it was something older, and he thought as he had given the laws he could both ignore them and withdraw them whenever he wanted.

This was why the Duma opened to find the Tsar still declaring himself an autocrat, still appointing the Ministers, still funding right-wing terror, able to dissolve the Duma at will and use emergency acts to pass laws. The Duma voters were weighted in favour of monarchists, and their actual power was very slim. They could not pass laws, just veto or propose them to the Tsar and his State Council of fossils (half voted for by top of society, half picked by the Tsar) and hope against hope he and they would agree and pass them, which he didn't over anything liberal.

And yet, the Duma was full of optimism, believing they had taken the first step to turning into the government of Britain or Revolutionary France. They didn't believe the Tsar would dare close this new body and try to ignore it. The world was watching! Investors were watching! There was a giant portrait of the Tsar in the chamber watching! People flocked from all corners of Russia to come to the Duma and present their problems and wishes. They were, as optimists tend to be, wrong.

The SRs and SDs decided to boycott the first set of elections, because they didn't consider a liberal talking shop right for them. This left the peasants to join the Labour party, which called for nothing less than a land reform that made large landowners unable to sleep. The Kadets were the biggest party, but this collection of representatives was unusual: they had a fair share of the Menshevik vote, and decided that as they'd just been elected to a Duma for the first time they should press ahead with demands of the Tsar. They thought this was the Estates General and it was time to get their constitutional assembly. They were going to oppose the Tsar, and they knew as the socialists were absent this was their chance to veer left and gain socialist support too. They believed they were on the cusp of leading a widely supported revolution to get a western constitution. There then followed one of the greatest snubs in the world's constitutional history.

The deputies of the new Duma sent the Tsar their demands: a government the Duma could affect, the end of the monarchist state council so the Duma could pass laws, land reform and every adult male getting the vote. The Tsar spent two weeks—well, the Duma thought he spent two weeks considering this—and then he replied with two things he was going to pass and would they vote on them: a new laundry, and a new greenhouse. You read that right, the Duma asked for vast constitutional reform and the Tsar sent back laws on minor buildings. It was a declaration of war.

The Duma pressed on, making demands. Unlike 1917, at this point the Kadets and Labour parties were trying to solve the land question by demanding major reform, including the removal and distribution of aristocratic holdings, and the current owners weren't exactly sympathetic.

Liberal Suicide

The result was, on July 8th, the dissolution of the first Duma followed by the appointment of a new Prime Minister, Stolypin. There was widespread outrage, and some of the Kadets decided to commit career suicide, for a large group of them ran to the Finnish town of Vyborg and issued a manifesto urging the people to rise up. Some did, and there were mutinies and peasant outrages, but nowhere near enough, because these Kadets had misread how keen people were to follow them, and they were arrested and banned from the Duma.

The effect of this was startling. The disillusion of Duma one was followed by elections for the second, and the Kadets who now went into the second and third Dumas were less radical, more inclined to compromise, because all the radical ones had just got themselves banned. More importantly, this marked the end of the liberals trying to solve the land question in a manner that appealed to the peasants. In 1917 we shall see the liberal government of Russia avoid the land question until it helped kill them. That started here. It was also broader: the people had not risen when the Kadets had asked, so they would stop appealing to the people, stop thinking they could herd the people. Into these gaps stepped other groups, like the Bolsheviks.

Stolypin: How To Lose Friends And Alienate People

We now meet one of the most remarkable men of the era, Petr Stolypin. You can tell he's remarkable, because everyone hated him at the same time. On the one hand, socialist opposition during his five years as Prime Minister (from 1906 to 1911) named the hangman's noose after him (Stolypin's necktie), as well as prison trains, such was his brutal approach to crushing peasant rebellion. The peasants were still attacking the wealthy, while a cult of terrorism was killing and wounding thousands of victims. The Tsar and the government weren't that keen on Stolypin's attempt to reform the country. He was a man who was proud of taking tough decisions, the sort which got him killed in a revenge attack. Historians ever since have wondered: had Stolypin lived, would he have been the only man in Russia willing to reform hard enough to avoid the civil war and the revolution, a series of actions that annoyed just about everyone? Did Nicholas II really come to rue the day he started fighting Stolypin instead of listening?

Stolypin is very much an example of the rule that if you attempt something big, it's better to die partway through so everyone misses you rather than living to see the inevitable failure. Stolypin was attempting to reform an ancient, autocratic regime full of dinosaurs, but keep it apart from the new, hungry anger of the mass of Russia, and he attempted this without getting the support of either. He attempted to walk a tightrope without getting the backing of the floor, the net or even the rope. Stolypin ended up being attacked from all sides, whereas if he'd at least cultivated a political party to support him, rather than carrying on a doomed hero figure, he might have stood a chance. Even Lenin had a party, and Lenin wasn't a remotely likable man. Stolypin tried, but failed.

How could Stolypin get into this position? The answer was the same one that drove his reform programme. Stolypin was a member of a government family, but he came from outside St. Petersburg. He rose through the ranks in provincial Russia, owning land and dealing with angry peasants, and in 1905 he took very strong action to put down the peasants and restore order, the sort of effective quelling of opposition that made the Tsar take notice, bring him into government, and then make him Prime Minister. But Stolypin hadn't just been arresting peasants, he had been looking at their anger, and he had decided Russia could only have a stable future if the peasant revolution was stopped, and that would only happen if he turned Russia's peasants into land-owning ones, western-style owners of their own private property. He was in many ways right with the theory, and knew the practice was going to involve much hard, if not suicidal work. He felt he was the man to do it. He wore a protective vest, had plenty of security and believed he'd be assassinated. He just hoped he could delay that long enough to make a difference. He was a dramatist who claimed to be brilliant, and he'd have to be. The Tsar and the government didn't want these changes, and the peasants saw a man who hanged them.

He launched into power with the stick of censoring newspapers, executing and exiling rebels, and slamming the Tsar's power back on top of the workers and peasants, which the Tsar liked but liberals were horrified with. Then he offered the carrot of reform: an end to village communes and the start of private property and civil rights, universal schooling, rights for workers and more. Not to be liberal, but to remove the props of revolution and leave the Tsar intact in a conservative but stable society.

A reformer, but not one who wanted a Duma. He wanted power to instead stay with the Tsar and him, so when

101

the 'Duma of National Anger' was voted in, he resolved to challenge it, which wasn't much of a shock to the newly elected 222 socialist deputies (all the main socialist parties had stood). Stolypin's answer was the sort of reform left-wingers didn't like, because he had the Duma dissolved and the voting laws changed to produce something more conservative in flavour. It worked, and the socialists and Kadets fared badly. But even tweaking voting laws and blatantly cheating couldn't produce a Duma which would do what Stolypin told it, as previously loyal groups like the Octobrists used their new-found Duma power to try and wrest some actual power off the state. Stolypin would find no solution in the Duma.

He wouldn't find one in the Tsar either. Nicholas liked chief ministers who did what they were told, who followed autocratic monarchs. He didn't want men turning up with vast peasant land reform at the expense of the gentry, even if it would stop a revolution. If you're thinking, well, Stolypin certainly seems autocratic material for the Tsar to like, the truth was Stolypin was at fundamental odds with the Tsar too, because for Stolypin it was the state who should have the massive powers, not the ancient royalty of the country. Or, Stolypin, not the Tsar, if you want to be a bit more cynical about it. Stolypin tried to stop the Duma taking power from the core state, and tried to take power for the core state from the Tsar. It's basically a miracle he lasted as long as he did, but he'd crushed the aftershocks of the 1905 revolution and had some space.

So: a proposal to increase state education blocked by interests of ancient churches who ran schools; a proposal to reform the police and make them state-controlled blocked by royalist police; local aristocrats savaging land reforms which tried to turn the peasants into citizens. People expected the political right to kill him as much as the left. On one issue, to extend government down to the rural level and enfranchise a whole new level of land-owning peasant citizens, the political right came together so hard he had to actually give up. Richard Pipes wonders if this reform would have slowed or even prevented the power vacuums in rural areas that marked 1917.

Stolypin was probably ruined before he was killed, and it happened over the Western Zemstvo Bill. The details of this act are a mixture of nationalism, cunning and conservative opposition, but suffice to say Stolypin thought he had a way to reform and develop zemstvos in Polish Russia, the bill was voted down by the State Council, Stolypin threatened to resign unless the Tsar closed the Duma and passed the bill using his emergency powers, and the Tsar did so. When the Duma was reopened, the deputies returned to their seats with surprisingly little complaint, a sign of why they lived out the full five-year term from 1907 to 1912.

Everyone seems to have been upset by what had happened. The liberals hated the Duma being treated like this (even though the changed voting rules made the third Duma a conservative bastion anyway). The Tsar seems to have felt personally wounded about ten minutes after agreeing to do it, and the peasants still weren't getting any land reform. Even Stolypin, the self-confident grandstander, thought he was ruined. In one of those Nelsonian gestures of suicide, Stolypin went to an area where the police told him there was an assassination plot, with no bodyguards and without his bulletproof vest, and was probably totally unsurprised that someone shot and killed him. No one ever really worked out whether the assassin was for the right or the left, because they ended up all hating him. We just know he was an SR (left) who worked for the police (right). The autopsy suggested that internal illness would have killed the disgraced Prime Minister soon anyway, while the fact the Tsar snubbed him at the theatre suggests his political career would have been over with similar speed.

Stolypin is a prime example of how strong-willed men cannot succeed in the modern world for long without support or political skills, and he never tried to create a party that would back him. He was the reform, and when he died there was no one to step in. No Stolypin party who kept pushing for a land-owning peasantry. Even Lenin thought that if Stolypin was successful the Bolsheviks would stand no chance of winning power. Did Stolypin's death rob Russia of the last, best chance for change?

In a word, no. Stolypin got nowhere near implementing any major changes, nowhere near mending the massive fault lines in Russian society. He had no realistic answer, and no way of making the riskier ones happen. He threw government money and agencies into a programme of enclosure, a word that strikes fear into the heart of industrial revolution students: peasants were encouraged to consolidate their scattered strips of land into more economic blocks, to use better methods, to basically westernise, develop and break free from the commune and the old system. Yet the old system fought back, and of all requests for government aid in enclosing land, a third were cancelled by the people who'd asked after pressure from their fellows. Stolypin died, and the reforms ground to a halt.

The Duma Declines, The Socialists Rise

This is going to sound pretty ridiculous, but things got worse for the Duma and they were already going badly. When we last saw them, Stolypin had managed to install a more conservative group of deputies, but even these collapsed in the voting for the fourth Duma and it limped along with no leadership, no voice, just a mish-mash of parties all arguing with each other and being ignored. Attendance fell, attempts to do things failed. It was a body in decline. But it was still hanging around for when a crisis might spring it into life. A World War One-shaped crisis.

What wasn't declining was socialist support—in fact this was rocketing thanks to some outright murderous brutality. Previous to this the security services had managed to get spies deep inside the socialists (two of the bosses of the Bolshevik paper *Pravda* and one on the central committee), while the Bolshevik and Mensheviks in exile argued over minutiae that meant precisely nothing to your average industrial worker being slowly killed by his boss. Then, in April 1912, a demonstration by mine workers on the Lena River turned into a state murder of five hundred of them, triggering a wave of ever-growing strikes over the next couple of years. Even more tellingly, this wasn't broad-based socialist support, because the Bolsheviks were outstripping the Mensheviks, taking control of key trade unions and becoming the most widely read (if not listened to) group. Having declined to nothing, events like the Lena River massacre, ever-more grassroots activists, and the strident tones of Lenin from abroad (a man who did not cease in his role) returned them to importance.

Also growing was a new Russian nationalism. This would lead to war.

Could the Duma have worked? English speakers tend to judge the Duma a failure, because they are used to different forms of government. But in terms of Russia, the Duma was a major advance, and the fact people could stand with freedom of speech and political immunity (well, in theory) and attack or question the Tsar played a large role in degrading the system of the Tsars. Richard Pipes makes an interesting observation in his history published in 1990: it wasn't Stolypin who could have fixed Russia. Had the members of the Duma been patient, started slowly and worked within the system, they might have stood a chance of effecting slow change. Instead, they turned up in 1906 and began to fight for more, immediately and bluntly. Would long-game subtlety have worked?

CRIB

- The first Duma is mainly liberals, and they go on the attack for more gains. The Tsar dismisses it.

- The second Duma is dominated by socialists, who are there to disrupt government. The Tsar dismisses it.

- A strongman leader is brought in, and he crushes rebellion. But Stolypin also tries to pass a massive reform programme, with the centrepiece an attempt to end the peasant commune and turn the peasantry into a class of land-owning farmers.

- Everyone starts to hate Stolypin, even the peasants who mostly reject ending the commune.

- After a final clash with the Tsar and a Duma, Stolypin allows himself to be assassinated.

- Russia then coasts into World War One, with socialist groups getting stronger.

7: World War One

In February 1914, a former Minister of the Interior called Durnova wrote to the Tsar to warn him that, if the tensions building in the Balkans led to war, the Russian state would inevitably fail to function, collapse, and be swept away by revolution. He couldn't have been more correct without naming Franz Ferdinand. But when the time came in 1914, when the continent was so far on the precipice of war that just a few leaders could decide yes or no, the Tsar was also told that refusing to fight would weaken him so much there would be collapse and revolution. The Tsar was given a stark choice: mobilise Russian troops and turn the Austro-Serbian war into a global conflict in which his control would cease, or refuse, and lose it all anyway. Nicholas II chose the option that killed the most people in a war fought for no good reason at all.

You may remember that in 1904 Russia became involved in a failed war with Japan, that caused an attempt at revolution in 1905. In 1914, Russia became involved in a war that failed on an entirely vaster scale, and caused an entirely more successful set of revolutions.

So, back to the run up to 1914.

A Desire for Empire

For centuries, Russia had lusted after the port of Constantinople and the straits through which a huge amount of Russia's trade passed to and from Europe, but they'd always faced the problem of the current owner: the Ottoman Empire. However, that state was now considered 'the sick man of Europe' and was starting to be torn into pieces by nationalist movements. The other great European neighbour of the Ottomans, the Austro-Hungarian Empire, was no less a polyglot being pulled apart by the spinning of nationalism, and a series of wars in the Balkans had seen countries emerge and stake their place.

Russia was looking lustfully at the Balkans too. Like many in Russia, the people in this area identified, or were identified, as Slavs, and the Russians felt they could expand their control into a Slavic Eastern European empire. Here they had always been stymied by the current owners, the Austrians, and Prussia (and now Germany) had loomed large too. But if Austria and the Ottomans were being weakened, if small states were forming, then surely (to many in Russia) the Slavic godfather should be their protector, if not their actual ruler? Serbia was expanding into a direct three-way struggle between two dying Great Powers and one who thought it was ready.

Russia had been allied with Germany under Bismarck, but by the 1910s Bismarck was long gone. Right wing critics in Russia, the people who normally supported the Tsar, demanded a Russian intervention in the Balkan wars, where Ottoman control was thrown off by Serbia and others. When Austria actually annexed Bosnia-Herzegovina in 1908, the Russian nationalists and pan-Slavists were livid with the government: how could they allow this to happen!

Russia versus Germans

As the pan-Slavists in Russia demanded action to defend their 'brothers', they also reacted against something else: pan-Germanism.

The Germans were going through essentially the same development as the Russians. Many on the right in Germany thought they should build a great Eastern empire at the expense of the Slavs, and replace its culture with Germany's imperial one. Stop me if this sounds oddly familiar. But the pan-Germans and pan-Russians knew about each other and reacted, both fearing the other would invade and bring destruction. Many in Germany felt a war with Russia was inevitable and wanted it while Germany had the advantage of superior industry. Germany wanted to take the Western Russian Empire for itself. Many in Russia felt a reckoning with the Germans was inevitable, and saw every insult in the Balkans as a starting point.

By the time of the Balkans Wars of 1912-13, the Tsar, the Court, the military and the government wanted to intervene in the Balkans, if only to use this nationalism to unite the people in an anti-German crusade. By early 1914 the Tsar seemed adamant Austria should be opposed. The question was, what about the much stronger Germany? Russia's military were telling the Tsar they needed to wait until 1917 to be ready to fight that rival empire.

Declaring War: World War One

When Austrian Archduke Franz Ferdinand was assassinated by a Serb terrorist, the former's emperor took a suspiciously long time to declare war on the latter, a time which betrayed exactly how cynical Austria's war was meant to be. Germany backed Austria up, and everyone looked to the Tsar. Nicholas II knew Russia would take a long time to mobilise due to bad transport, and needed to make a quick decision. Many elites in Russia demanded action to defend the Slav Serbs. After an appeal to the Kaiser of Germany, Nicholas ordered the mobilization of Russia on July 31st. World War One was inevitable.

At first the people united, as they tend to do. Flags were waved by all orders. Strikes ended. Germans were beaten up by mobs. Such was the patriotic insanity that St. Petersburg was deemed too German a name, and it became Petrograd, while the Duma dissolved itself so it didn't bother the Tsar during the war.

Initial Success

It started well for Russia. They had been spending huge sums on modernising their army and getting ready for this European war, and while they were still three years away from peak performance (well, in theory), a lot had been done. Railway developments meant Russia mobilized almost as quickly as the Germans, whose plan was designed to take advantage of a much slower enemy. But Russia weren't slow, moving west at such speed the Schlieffen Plan – which wasn't much of a plan to start with, more some vague notes that somehow got turned into the start of a war – was ruined and the Central Powers found themselves fighting on two sides. Germany was fighting the war it had feared, two simultaneous fronts, with the Russians in the east and the British and French in the west. It was a disaster for the Kaiser, as his eastern forces were only one eighth of the Germany army, the rest being used to attack the French.

The Russians were prepared for a six-month campaign, which was true of every nation, and had once planned to defend their north-west border against the Germans while pushing south-west into the weaker Austrians and the Slavic lands towards the Serbia they were meant to be helping. The Russian army was better trained and equipped than later legend, and they were moving fast thanks partly to French money for railways, so they happily accepted a French request to attack north-west too. This would take the pressure off France, who were facing the bulk of the German attack. On the Austrian front Brusilov, the premier Russian commander of the war, broke through in the south and pushed the Austrians back 130 miles.

The German front was a disaster. The Germans were supposed to be holding the Russians off until France was beaten. Two Russian armies advanced, aiming to combine at the Masurian Lakes and then push to Berlin. They dithered, wasting time and resources, but they still pushed the Germans back, causing panic in German high command, and wasted this chance by dithering once more. The Germans replaced their commanders with an old legend and a new thinker, Hindenburg and Ludendorff, and then it went wrong for Russia. Spectacularly wrong. Hindenburg and Ludendorff were able to use an astonishing fact to their advantage: the Russians had been sending messages uncoded. The Germans could read them all. In twentieth century warfare, that was about as bad as running out of guns and bullets at the same time (don't worry, that happens in a minute).

Rapid Failure

The Germans knew exactly where the Russians were, and the Russians had no idea of the opposite. When the

114

Germans read one of the two Russian armies had stopped for supplies, they moved the bulk of their troops on their excellent railway network and defeated the other army so soundly and successfully the Russian commander shot himself. Russia lost nearly two hundred thousand men and the chance to win the war in the six months they planned. Had Russia realized, they could have reacted and won the war by surging through areas left open (the Germans had almost all been pulled to the other battle), but they sat and were, in one of those rare moments in military history, exactly where the Germans wanted them. Following this 'Battle of Tannenberg' (named to avenge a medieval battle Germans had lost, because at this point in the war that sort of thing seemed a good idea), Germany used the railways and reinforcements from the western front to attack the remaining Russian army … and it fled backwards. Another sixty thousand died.

When the lines stabilized defensive warfare began, and several problems became evident. Firstly, Russian commanders cared nothing for the mounting cost in lives, and the rank and file knew it. Morale collapsed, patriotism vanished, and the soldiers looked to other ideologies for help … like socialism. More problematical was an issue all belligerents faced: how to turn an army (and a country) designed for a short war into a nation able to fight a total war

115

over many years. Germany, France and Britain all met this challenge. Russia failed it utterly, as the old system proved incapable of adaption. Russia had more people, but fewer of them were the right age and job to serve in the military; to save money reserves had not been trained. Russia, the sinkhole of Napoleon and Hitler, ran out of trained soldiers early and struggled to make it up. The Germans would mobilise over ten per cent of their population in this war, while Russia didn't get to half that. When soldiers were provided they were largely peasants who cared little for a war of imperial gain outside their own village. March to Berlin or Constantinople? No. They were not high in morale. Command was also bad. The leading commanders were aristocrats or court favourites, with little experience or ability. Some were actually incompetent. The skilled were stuck below them. The whole command was divided into competing elements, meaning there was no unified plan. Even Brusilov, the proven success, was considered an outsider of less than servile loyalty.

Abject Failure

This translated into bad orders, bad strategy, bad tactics and a reluctance to invest in proper trenches in a war all about defence. People were slaughtered because their defences weren't good enough, and slaughtered when ordered to charge at German defences which were. Command did not care about

116

the losses. Transport ground to a halt, as the system was overwhelmed and their trains wouldn't run on German rails. The ports were either blockaded, frozen or didn't even have any rail links (step forward Murmansk for that gem). An obsession with cavalry sucked up resources. Communications were a vast failure, and then Russia ran out of supplies, guns and ammunition. Soldiers were restricted to ten rounds a day, if they still had a gun, which they sometimes had to fetch from the dead in front of them. Now it was Russia's turn to make no provisions for winter clothing, believing they would only be fighting for six months and now sending soldiers out without coats or boots. Cold and hunger was followed by disease, always a terrible killer of soldiers. Officers were killed by annoyed troops. Soon the bulk of the army had awful morale and little in the way of loyal officers. It became revolutionary, as annoyed soldiers from working class and peasant backgrounds were promoted and took their dissatisfaction with them. As millions of men were called up, officers ran out before they even got to the casualties. The old-school command got the best supplies and often stayed at the back while ordering lethal attacks. The soldiers hated this class–military division and became a revolutionary mass crying out for an end to war and to be treated like humans, with a newly created class of NCO to lead them. When the soviets came, the soldiers welcomed them.

In May 1915, the Germans attacked, having moved most of their army to the area in an attempt to knock Russia out and hope France conceded; Russia folded, but did not quit. Pushed back, they found a defensive stand negated because all the equipment had been either sold off for profit or lost, and they were forced to retreat into Russia. This meant Brusilov and his success in the south-west was destroyed as he had to retreat or else be surrounded. More German advances easily took old fashioned fortresses defended with old fashioned techniques but piled high with supplies. The high command fooled itself this was 1812 all over again and the modern Napoleons would face the same fate. In reality it was chaos. Soldiers fled past destroyed stores of things they needed. Rumours began of traitors and spies in government, including the Tsarina and the generals. Soon, over ten percent of the Russian Empire's population was now in a German zone of occupation. France and Britain should celebrate the error the Germans made in wasting a year on this front, before the Germans turned back west. The Russians, however, walked into an abyss by doing so.

The Tsar Takes Control

Now the Tsar acted in a way that destroyed him. Facing utter military collapse, on August 22nd he announced he would take over as supreme commander from Grand Duke

118

Nikolai and move to Mogilev to command. He thought the army would fight for its Tsar. The problem was the Tsar didn't have a clue how to fight, or organise an army, so he became personally associated with the many failures. Also, he left central government behind and that descended into chaos too. Rasputin fired and hired government officials for bribes and whims. Russian command became a joke. Not only was the government and the military failing, but the Tsar had ensured he would be seen to fail with it. For centuries the tsars had created an image of the gruff godfather who defended the normal people against grasping elites, and now from 1905 to this, he had become a flawed, useless laughing stock. The stupid thing was, even at the front he didn't organise strategy, and his own ministers appealed to him not to go. He just watched and got all the blame. The Tsarina, as usual the forceful, decisive one, said the opposite—although to be fair to her, her initiative to transform the noble women of Russia into a medical corps was doing better than the actual military, who began the war with just two motor ambulances. Not two per unit, two in total.

The Second State

How did Russia survive into 1917? Private forces. Lvov headed a massively expanded zemstvo union which, with other bodies and volunteers, kept the war running. A second government emerged, one which could find and send supplies, one which had able, energetic people. Food was sourced sent out, the sick returned and treated, money rounded up and used. An entire class of Russia banded together in a second state that did actually work. It became clear that Lvov was doing better than the Tsar. People began to say the Tsar should just hand over control full stop.

Many in government were opposed to this state, and actually tried to hinder and stop it, so Lvov radicalized, saying the people were governing themselves and deserved a constitution when the war ended. The liberals in Russia, who had wanted to stay loyal to the Tsar, were going with him, all annoyed, all frustrated, all willing to demand change. The Tsar's government struggled to repel criticism, even sacking people (and arresting the War Minister). Other bodies formed in opposition, such as business leaders determined to break government given monopolies and kickbacks to friendly firms, which were costing money and producing little. All these groups made a web between them of reform, opposition and demands.

The Tsar finally agreed to a Duma recall in mid-1915, and a Progressive Bloc consisting of liberal parties formed, aiming to stop revolution by gaining concessions over government. Two thirds of the Duma joined the block, and efforts were made to promote the reforms in a manner the Tsar would agree with. A group of government ministers came together and asked the Tsar to listen, and they published a carefully worded document which enthused the middle class. The Tsar decided not to repeat the 'mistake' of 1905 and closed the Duma again, informing everyone he would rule as an autocrat. He was in charge, and he didn't want any credit won by the second state. It was the tragedy of Russia that he was inept too. Ministers who had supported the progressive bloc were sacked. With autocracy reinforced and the Tsar at the front (relatively speaking), the Tsarina caused chaos with four prime ministers, three war ministers, four interior ministers all appointed in seventeen months, among others. All at her whim, which was obeying the whim of the unelected, messianic figure, Rasputin. Some of these were able men, and one of them. Polivanov, had saved the Russian army from destruction through his organization; he was replaced by a man who once noted "I may be a fool, but I am no traitor," and I assure you I'm not making that up. It's very easy to accuse the Tsarina of mishandling the situation (because she did), but Alan Wood looked at her letters and said she was in a state of "psychotic dementia". Richard Pipes carries on his criticism of the liberals and socialists by arguing the Tsar did give concessions (seemingly in deigning to work with the private sector at all) and the Duma just kept demanding more and more.

The power of Duma politics was clear for all to see: there was none. Nothing nice was getting through to the Tsar or the Tsarina, the situation was politically bankrupt. People would need to be more extreme. But the liberals were terrified that would unleash the workers or the peasants, who they didn't trust to do anything beyond start a bloody anarchy. The nation limped on, waiting. However, even the government needed to do something about the war, and it allowed the creation of special councils which included business people and experts as well as government officials to organise production. In one of the more remarkable episodes, the Military-Industrial Committee invited (what turned out to be Menshevik) workers to assist. This was a first, and showed there was a potential way through, but it was kept small.

The Brusilov Offensive

Plans were made for an attack. Brusilov, now promoted, had been trying to improve his army, had been learning the lessons of the war, and volunteered to make an assault to support his fellow commanders. Told he would have no new supplies or men, he planned a proper offensive using what he had. His fellows thought him mad, but Brusilov was a genius who hatched a plan that reflected what he could realistically attain. Models of enemy trenches were built in total secrecy to train on, and the attack would not be dependent on interior railways. The Brusilov Offensive began on June 4th, and was an initial success, breaking through to capture 200,000 enemies, such a blow to the Austrian forces they were considering a surrender. Had the other Russian commanders attacked as they should, Germany would have been in real trouble, but they refused, too afraid, and the Tsar wouldn't order it. So Brusilov pushed on, unsupported, and Germany and Austro-Hungary were able to use their superior railways to concentrate on it. The offensive came to a halt, and Brusilov turned against the Tsar. The most successful Russian commander, a royalist, saw that the royals stood in the way of victory.

Russia Falls Apart

Inflation (you couldn't afford what was available), lack of supplies (little was available), rising crimes (someone stole what was available once you'd afforded it): the cities of the home front were falling apart. Revolution was openly spoken of, elites partied as if they were doomed. Millions of soldiers were based in cities on their way to being thrown into the meatgrinder, placing two large and upset groups near each other. The urban population of Russia rose by millions in just two years. People thought the Tsarina, Rasputin and even the Tsar were working for the Germans. The royal family became 'German', hated by a 'patriotic' Russian people. The workers

123

and the peasants began to turn against the Duma too, seeing it as useless, which it was. Liberals began to think their fear of a working class, socialist revolt would be reduced by moving from old problems to meeting the socialists halfway: not working with the government, but bringing their own government in instead. A liberal revolution that would stop socialism. Everyone was growing desperate. The air was turning violent.

The Duma assembled on November 1st, 1916, and the government was asked if its failures were folly or treason by a man called Miliukov. This went wrong as Miliukov had meant for everyone to conclude folly, while everyone actually concluded treason, which was vastly more damaging. The Kadets fought a verbal war in order to concede they would not attempt to charge the government with treason, itself a revolutionary idea and act.

Many, even conservatives, now thought some revolution necessary. The Tsar was not conceding enough, if anything. The working class and peasants seemed to not just be against the Tsar, but increasingly didn't think the Duma would do anything either, so they'd have to do it themselves. Two rivers of revolution began to flow. The Duma liberals determined to act before Tsar and socialists both destroyed the nation, and the socialists, feeling the liberals were no help, were going to act on their own. Even the elites, worried about a revolution, wanted to act and create a safe Russia for themselves. Everyone except a very small royal circle wanted change, and not just change but revolution—albeit they all wanted a different type. Rasputin was murdered by angry nobles, and people spoke of abducting the Tsar or royals to build new structures around them. Even Lvov, zemstvo man Lvov, sounded out a plot to replace the Tsar with a more able royal (the target royal, Grand Duke Nikolai Nikolaevich, declined to mention anything to the Tsar). Everyone knew something was going to happen. Royalist elites were siding with liberals, socialists were seething. The Tsar even replaced his Prime Minister with someone the liberals liked and left the Duma in session complaining. Historians like Pipes complain the Russian intelligentsia should have worked with this, and not allowed February 1917 to progress. It's hard to see how they could have.

The Socialists

The Mensheviks were divided between people who wanted to support the Russian government in winning the war, and those more interested in a Russian or even European revolution. The same was true of the SRs: some were 'patriots' in the imperial cause, others were internationalists wanting peace and socialist change. Many Mensheviks pushed for acknowledging the right of Russia to self-defence, while leading lights like Martov called for an end to war and a settlement with 'no annexations or indemnities' and a map redrawn on national self-determination, which was precisely the opposite of what imperial nations like Germany, France and the UK were fighting for (and which Russia had been too).

Bolsheviks, however, were mostly united under Lenin's call for pan-European revolution, a war against war, the people rising up against the imperial slaughter they had been sent to. Lenin went even further: the war must not be fought by the common soldier against Germany, but they must contest a civil war against the Tsar. Lenin was a fringe player in a fringe group, and was in exile, as were many of the professional revolutionaries. These leading revolutionaries did not win the war for hearts and minds and socialist support. What won that was the working class seeing everything happening and mostly failing so turning against the Tsar.

Then the economy failed. Inflation was rampant, workers struggled to get food causing upset, while production of grain for sale fell and transport favoured the military, leaving foodstuffs rotting in sidings. Ordinary people went hungry. The government tried to forcefully take grain from scared peasants, alienating them, and banned the sale of vodka while leaving expensive spirits for themselves. Queues for food grew, and the people in them talked and ranted against the Tsar, spending hours with nothing to do but get worked up. Strikes spread, starting with demands for bread and ending with demand for the abdication of the Tsar. These weren't led by leading Mensheviks, Bolsheviks or others, these were organic and growing.

The Germans knew this was happening, and were spending large sums of money on influencing and encouraging revolutionary groups in Russia. Soon they would go further by depositing Lenin there.

Richard Pipes is confident enough to blame the collapse of the Russian government on an aspect of this war, but not the one you might think. In a fascinating conclusion in his large history of the Russian Revolution, he pins what happens next not on the failures of the autocratic system, but on the lack of a universal sense of Russian togetherness: "Russia's collapse in 1917 and withdrawal from the war was due, first and foremost to political causes – namely, the unwillingness of government and opposition to bury their differences in the face of a foreign enemy. The absence in Russia of an overriding sense of national unity was never more painfully in evidence." (Pipes, 1990, 209) As I hope this book has shown, I have placed the blame far more on the government than the people.

In January 1917, Lenin showed that while he might end up in charge, he was as capable as everyone else at being

127

incorrect, telling friends he and other older revolutionaries might not live to see a Russian Revolution. He was proved wrong with startling alacrity.

CRIB

- Pan-Slavic demands, nationalism and good old fashioned imperial greed mean Russia felt obliged to meddle in the Balkans.

- When Austria declared war on Serbia in 1914, the Tsar was warned that joining this war would destroy him, but that not joining would do the same. He declared war, escalating a local conflict into the global World War One.

- The Russian war effort failed to win a quick victory, and the Russian state wasn't able to adapt to a war of attrition. Supply, production, morale and belief all broke down.

- The liberals were able to organise more effectively than the Tsarist state and helped the war last.

- Slowly, faced with the utter failure of the Tsar, his government and a lack of compromise, huge numbers of Russians believed a revolution was necessary to survive, including the royal elites.

- The military, defenders in 1905, lost faith in the Tsar.

8: The February Revolution

The February Revolution of 1917 was not started by some grand communist ideal. The fact we have a Lenin-led Soviet Union at the end of this book meant nothing in February. In fact, the February Revolution didn't start from any grand ideas at all, be they desires for a constitution, democracy or socialist utopia. The trigger for the revolution was far simpler, far more universal. The trigger was food and heat. If you're in charge of a troubled nation, never underestimate the impact of food.

A transport network that had started off faulty was focused on the military, degrading in war rather than being replaced. In February 1917 a particularly cold and snowy winter frequently brought transport to a standstill, meaning that flour and fuel could not get to Petrograd (as St. Petersburg was now called to make people feel patriotic and fluffy) in sufficient amounts at the same time to feed everyone. It wasn't enough to just get flour in (indeed, there were stores of it in the city) because you needed to fuel to bake it, and the symbiotic system was broken.

People were hungry, and that led to anger. Violence occurred as people fought over supplies. The bitter winter pulled on the fuel supply. The women of Petrograd had to queue all night for bread, usually to be told that there wasn't enough, while men increasingly found themselves laid off because the transport problems meant factories stopped, unable to bring in raw materials or move out products. The result was a city with large numbers of hungry, cold, unemployed people with nothing to do, able to share rumours and blame, accusing German merchants or Germans in government of trying to destroy the people. The city government declared on February 19th that rationing would begin March 1st, but escalating gossip turned this into the fake fact that the unemployed would not be fed and every bakery in the city was soon sold out from panic. Then the weather changed, and it was balmy enough for a mass protest. It would stay warm(ish) for a crucial period.

The Revolution Begins

On February 23rd, 1917, International Women's Day, a mass women's march gathered to march for after equal rights. It was organized by grassroots socialists. Thanks to a general, all-encompassing dissatisfaction with Russia, the Vyborg textile women also marched, in a protest over bread shortages, and they were joined by striking men. More and more came out to protest. Soon 100,000 workers had flooded out. As Vyborg workers tried to get to the centre of the city, they were stopped by police, and most went home. But thousands used the ice to cross the river, met with the women of Women's

Day, and merged. Cossacks were sent to break up this crowd, albeit with orders not to start a street war. The Cossacks didn't use large-scale violence, and the crowd noted how reluctant they seemed to be in even a limited role. The crowd's demands had changed from equal rights to bread, and then to 'down with the tsar'. Inside the Duma, politicians launched scathing attacks on the government. For historian Richard Pipes, who takes a dim view of socialist revolution, these politicians inflamed the street and behaved irresponsibly.

On February 24th, workers across the city gathered and decided to march to the centre and carry the protest on. They took weapons to counter the police and to loot food. That morning 150,000 workers came out, forcing police and shop windows aside. They gathered in the Nevsky Prospect. Cossacks were charging the protestors but stopping without any contact, and protestors were quickly regrouping and moving forward, allowing the march to continue. The workers were now swelled with thousands of students and shop staff, and the atmosphere was fun and socialist. Speakers used Tsarist symbols as focal points to speak from, appearing to conquer the old culture by standing on top of it speaking about a new one.

On February 25th, with the crowd feeling they had beaten the government's ability to stop them, a practical general strike brought between two hundred and three hundred thousand people onto the street. Red flags appeared and revolution was openly spoken of. Demands for bread were replaced with calls for the end of the war and the Tsar. The police tried to stop this march but were swept aside. Violent clashes began all over Petrograd, but the military sat, unwilling to intervene. The people saw the police as agents of government (and so the enemy), but the military as workers or peasants like them and therefore allies. The soldiers agreed. High theatre occurred at the Nevsky Prospect, where Cossacks who seemed about to charge with genuine violence (it that must have petrified those who remembered 1905) were brought round by a small girl who approached and offered flowers. They were accepted by the troops in a way a Hollywood movie wouldn't even get away with. Some soldiers fought, but many took a conscious decision to act differently from 1905, and this is the key, this is the change. Some soldiers even began to fight the police to defend protestors.

At this point local socialist leaders didn't believe a revolution was happening. Local Bolshevik leader Alexander Shliapnikov's on the street assessment was that giving workers each a pound of bread would have caused everyone to go home. There wasn't anything on this scale in any other city in Russia. This might not have been a revolution. Here was a crossroads, not an inevitable event, with people on the ground in a hunger riot. Enter the Tsar to mismanage the situation totally, as he ordered a military crushing of the rebellion. To be fair to the Tsar, he was misinformed. He was near the front (which was his poor choice), and the reports he'd been sent from his capital had been written to down-play the seriousness of the situation. He thought he had a nut and a hammer.

Even so, on February 26th the army was brought out onto the streets, with defended positions and machine guns. The people marched, the army opened fire, people died. The crowd was emboldened to not run away and episodes of violence occurred across the city. It was Bloody Sunday again. But then something changed. Soldiers began to fight other soldiers to stop massacres. Even some who had shot and killed demonstrators changed their minds as it all sank in. Just when things seem to have become repressed that evening, even allowing a major society ball to be held in comfort, it stopped being like Bloody Sunday because something new and vital happened: the military revolted in huge numbers.

The Military Joins In

On February 27th, lower ranking officers, not of the upper and elite class, led a mutiny of the Petrograd garrison. Kept in cramped conditions, treated brutally, soon to be sent to the pointless trenches of World War One, these largely peasant soldiers didn't want to fight other Russians, certainly not civilians with whom they agreed. With whom they felt one. The troops of the Petrograd Garrison either changed sides or sat on their hands and let it happen.

It was now a revolution, and the Tsar had lost control of the Russian capital. The reborn city was full of soldiers and workers capturing arms and key points, with tens of thousands of weapons being brought onto the streets. All the Tsar had was the police, who were now fighting a war against their own military. Prisons were opened, police stations burned (along with the files of criminals), people wore red symbols and waved red flags. The people managed to organise and react, yet they were doing it without the major socialist leaders, who were following what was happening from outside or were trapped in far-off isolation rather than leading. This was not their revolution. The organisers were lower ranking men and women now lost to history.

Once the prisons opened, the carnival atmosphere of the revolution changed into one of nasty violence and chaos. Many people died; people were robbed and raped, statues smashed, police lynched, a spontaneous reaction to the oppression of the Tsar. The February Revolution is often presented as bloodless, but it really wasn't. Years of repression and anger were now let loose, and like a volcano which had built enough force to erupt, the explosion and flinging of debris caused great damage.

The Soviet Forms

On the 27th, the more senior socialist leaders in the city finally caught up with what was going on. A crowd of 25,000 (mostly soldiers) formed outside the Tauride Place, home of the Duma, and saw the arrival of Menshevik leaders just freed from prison by the crowd. They brought with them a plan that changed history. These socialist intellectuals announced the Provisional Executive Committee of the Soviet of Workers Deputies, and ordered workers to elect representatives for the first meeting later that day. This first gathering had barely any time to organise, only fifty delegates, and they formed an Executive Committee of fifteen Mensheviks, Bolsheviks, SRs and other socialists. It's important to point out that this fifty, and especially this fifteen, weren't workers, but the intellectual, professional revolutionaries rather than the people they claimed to represent. As the real workers then realized this existed, they voted in six hundred soviet deputies, and more intellectuals were added to an expanded Executive Committee. It wasn't the workers and soldiers voting for an executive, but an executive forming to take control of the socialist movement. But only of the movement. The executive were people who didn't want to seize overall power in Russia, a fact that might surprise anyone who thought the socialists grabbed their chance with both hands. In addition, the votes and the elected people were overwhelmingly for moderate socialists like the Mensheviks. Extremes like the Bolsheviks had little support.

You might be expecting the mass of the soviet to be electing named people to the executive to represent them, but the Executive Committee had, by agreement of the senior intellectuals, formed in a different way: leading socialist parties had a set number of people on it, and they were chosen by the party. Basically, socialist leaders jockeyed for the executive committee, and the soviet jockeyed to be listened to.

The first meeting was poorly organized chaos, but as solders arrived to have a say a decision was made: this soviet would unite workers and soldiers, and the Petrograd Soviet of Workers and Soldiers Deputies was christened. But there were many more workers than soldiers in the area, and yet soldiers filled the soviet. For workers, they had just been eclipsed by the smaller number of better organized troops. In just a few days, socialist intellectuals supported by armed soldiers had cut out the voice of the workers, and then the intellectuals in the executive cut out the views of the soldiers. The grassroots socialist rebellion of late February had been hijacked. The streets and the Duma would look to each other uneasily.

The Duma Reacts

It wasn't all socialism, very far from it. At first, many people looked to the Duma and the Duma ducked and failed them.

The Tsar had ordered the Duma shut and its members were debating doing this, or refusing and trying to lead the revolution. Socialists in the Duma said lead it, while the middle ground said wait and see (as they were afraid of the 'mob' and didn't know how to control them). Those on the other extreme said the letter of the law forbid them from forming a new government but why not ask the Tsar nicely if he would just happen to allow that? Arguments raged. If the Duma went into rebellion against the Tsar, would they end up in a socialist state instead of their own government? That terrified liberals, but it became apparent that many, many people were looking to the Duma to form a new government, and every hour they waited the soviet was taking over, so a half-hearted compromise was reached. A handful of liberals, plus even fewer Duma socialists like Kerensky (who will soon become a major figure in this narrative), formed a Temporary Committee of Duma Members for the Restoration of Order in the Capital and the Establishment of Relations with Individuals and Institutions to promote order. We'll call it the TCD, and it wasn't the Duma acting, just a few people in the Duma doing something easily denied by the bulk of the rest. Nevertheless, when that night a soviet was meeting, and when

138

Grand Duke Mikhail turned down the call for a dictator, the TCD declared itself as the government for fear of the Soviet doing the same. In the city, Petrograd had strongpoints and the military was now organized by the Military Commission, which moved from Soviet to TCD control.

Not only Russia, but even just the Tauride Place now had two rival governments, the liberal TCD and the Soviet. In theory, the former spoke for the Duma and continuation of government, while the latter spoke for workers and soldiers. In practice, neither did. But they both had to try and take initiative and control. The TCD was trying to bring peace and order 'back to the street', to have an orderly revolution and not an apocalypse of violence. This meant ordering the arrest of Tsarist officials to save them from the mob! The Soviet had pretty much the same aim, as they wanted control, not to be riding a tsunami of blood.

This three-way power struggle of left and right and anarchy over the streets was clear when it came to the army, because the Duma wanted soldiers back in their barracks rather than causing trouble, but the soldiers feared a return to the old system if they went, believing the Duma too close to the elite officers. To that end, they were roaming around, patrolling and defending when they wanted and causing trouble when they didn't. This left the Soviet to try a solution: issue Order Number One. Soldiers were to have their own soviets, to obey only the Petrograd Soviet and not the Duma, to have rights and powers like not having to salute if off duty and not being glorified serfs. Soldiers were only to obey the TCD if appropriate. This was welcomed by soldiers when announced and at a stroke destroyed the cohesion of the Russian army. Order Number One wasn't about soldiers freeing themselves from officers or elites, it was about socialist intellectuals taking control of the soldiers and removing their counter-revolutionary threat.

The soviet now had an upper hand. They could have taken power, as they had a vast city following them. But the soviet didn't want to take power. They wanted a Duma-led bourgeois government. The people on the streets didn't, they wanted the soviet in charge. Again and again in 1917, starting with this moment, the Petrograd Soviet backed away from taking power, until the socialists in the city gave up and flocked to the Bolsheviks, a group who were willing to take power and wield it in a far more extreme way than the men of February might have.

Why did the socialists like the Mensheviks and SRs want liberals in power? Partly old socialist theory that a peasant nation like Russia wasn't ready for soviet rule: a bourgeois-led capitalist revolution was first needed to transform Russia to be ready for socialism. This oddity of thought was the fault of Marx, and of every Russian socialist

140

who believed him. They also thought peasants were still too resistant to an urban rebellion, wouldn't support it and would cause it to fail (in fact peasants wanted revolution as much as the workers if it meant a solution to the land question). People also considered peasants too uneducated to run a state yet. What Russia needed, these snobbish and blinkered socialists thought, was for Russia to simmer under liberal capitalism. This looks foolish now and often masks a second layer: the soviet leaders were trying to avoid all the blame if the revolution failed.

However, the truth was that socialist leaders had spent so long in small opposition groups they couldn't adapt to the chance to rule and were terrified: they feared a civil war with the Tsar and liberals that would destroy them. They were obsessed with the failures elsewhere in Europe of 1871 and 1848, and feared workers would not listen to them. They feared their own inability to think and adapt and rule, and they also feared for their lives. They were an opposition, not a political government. Only Lenin thought he was the leader.

The Provisional Government

On March 1st, the minority left wing of the Petrograd Soviet Executive Committee (which included the Bolsheviks) demanded the formation of a government from the soviet. The majority right wing had, as discussed, different desires, namely a liberal Duma government so socialism could cook for longer. The majority in the soviet worried that if something wasn't done soon, the left wing and the people on the street might undercut them and form their own soviet government, and even the dithering intellectuals on the right could agree they didn't want to lose their position. The TCD, meanwhile, wanted a Duma government and the soviet to take direction to calm the street. Therefore, that night, the leaders of the soviet entered into discussion with the TCD and an alliance, a dual government, was talked into being: all wanted order back, all wanted a Duma government. Those who wanted the Tsar dropped their calls in the face of cold reality.

With an agreement reached, the Duma began to form a government and the soviet supported it under a list of conditions which included political amnesties, free speech, the organization of a Constituent Assembly to write a constitution and a promise, which will become very important, not to send the troops of the capital who supported the revolution to the front of World War One. They would stay and defend revolution (and not fight the Germans).

This might sound good, but, critically, the alliance fudged two of the absolute key issues: the war situation (what to do with the demand to end it), and land (what to do with peasant demand for it). As we will see, it never managed to solve these issues and they helped destroy the alliance as the

142

Duma and the Soviets thought different things and neither had the will or power to act anyway. A Provisional Government was established, avoiding the main issues, allowing the soviets to have influence but no responsibility, the Duma unable to act without the soviets. If this sounds like a huge mess, that's because it was. It was hamstrung from the start. The eight-point agreement also dissolved the police and said a militia would replace it, and universal suffrage elections would be held for local government bodies. As you might expect, the first one caused anarchy and the second one chaos.

On March 2nd a cabinet was selected. Prince Lvov, the Duma man, the zemstvo man, became first Prime Minister and Minister of the Interior. He was respected by liberals, famous over Russia, but his nature as a prince limited his popularity on the street. He was kind, caring and totally unsuited to the bitter politics that were swirling around. Real power was in the right- and left-wing ministers like Miliukov and Kerensky, who orbited around Lvov and had interest in the top spot. Kerensky was the only socialist in the Provisional Government, and was also vice chairman of the Soviet Executive Committee. He'd managed to become the Provisional Government's Minister of Justice, despite the soviet officially staying out of this government in order to just accept or reject its work. It was a blurred, confused setup and Kerensky's ego was riding above it. Having been the sole joint member of the Soviet Executive Committee and the TDC, Kerensky carried on in his strange position of half-liberal, half (sort of) revolutionary. But he was highly popular with the people, just left enough for the left, just right enough for the right. You will see him rise even further in the next few chapters, as he wrapped himself in the revolution.

The End of the Tsar

At the Tsar's headquarters, he was living a fantasy life in a doomed daze. Only after several days of dismissing reports as exaggerations designed to boost the Duma did he realise how Petrograd was really rebelling. The order he gave on the 27th to use troops and crush the revolution was accompanied by the Tsar trying to take a train to Petrograd, against all advice, to aid his family. On March 1st his train arrived at Malaya Vishera and had to redirect because there was a revolution ahead, so it moved to Pskov. This took the Tsar away from his wife, whose bloody-minded determination might have affected the coming abdication. However, the crushing wasn't going well as the officers were either paralysed and overcome, or afraid the troops would refuse and the army would revolt. The Imperial Guard showed signs of rebellion, so the Tsar was stuck on a railway with his army leaving him and everyone too afraid to fight in case civil war began and the Germans marched in too.

The Duma decided to ask the Tsar to abdicate in favour of his son, deciding that a new figurehead was needed, and sent a team. Then the head of the army called a halt to any 'counterrevolution' because he had been promised that if he stopped and got the Tsar to quit, the liberals would form the new government, not the socialists, and there would be no risk of Russia losing World War One due to socialist soldiers and politicians quitting (which is actually what finally happens in 1918). The Generals then discussed what to do. At first, Nicholas finally listened to the few people he respected, his Generals, and conceded that the Duma could form a government. However, it soon became apparent to the Generals that this was too late, that Petrograd, the war and maybe even Russia could only be saved by stronger concessions. They told the Tsar to abdicate, Grand Duke Nicholai joined in, all telling him the only way to keep Russia intact and Germany out was for him to go. He could have signed an armistice with Germany and turned loyal front-line troops to the east, but even for him this would have been too much. For him, Russia had to win the war. For him, the military was everything.

The Tsar had spent years ignoring advice, but now the army was uniting against him. The Tsar thus abdicated, his bloody-minded desire to live as an autocrat in the mould of his father having doomed him. This was actually before the Duma representatives arrived to find it had already happened. At first Nicholas abdicated in favour of his son, but then considered his family: his son was sick and he didn't want to be parted from him in exile, and so Nicholas abdicated on behalf of both of them in favour of his brother, Grand Duke Mikhail. This was actually illegal in one sense, but as the Tsar could do what he liked as supreme autocrat, in another very real sense it wasn't really. Either way, no one at the time cared. The Duma looked at the mood on the street, decided they didn't want any monarchy and tried to talk the Grand Duke into abdicating too (not a hard job, which was followed by Nicholas II trying to abdicate again in favour of his son, an action that was entirely ignored). The right wing of the Provisional Government had wanted the monarchy to stay and build round; Kerensky wanted it gone or else face probable civil war and most people agreed with him. The Grand Duke, afraid for his life, quit. The three-century Romanov rule of Russia was over. The protective but stern father-Tsar was finally gone. Many people rejoiced, in cities and peasant communes across Russia.

CRIB

- Russia's Tsar and government are critically undermined by the war going badly.

- When a broken transport system can't take food and fuel to Petrograd, marches and strikes begin and spread.

- The Tsar orders soldiers to crush the strikers, but unlike 1905 soldiers start joining the strikers en masse because they are disaffected by the war.

- Petrograd's soldiers and workers rise in rebellion.

- A soviet forms, run by intellectuals 'on behalf' of workers and soldiers. It doesn't want to become the Russian government.

- A breakaway group of Duma men forms, and it declares itself the government.

- The Soviet and Duma ally, the latter agreeing to support the former when possible, and a Provisional Government is created.

- The Tsar's Generals refuse to march on Petrograd and ask him to abdicate; he does so. Royal rule ends.

- The Provisional Government, with Prince Lvov as Prime Minister, is now in official charge, but has to work with the Soviet in this confused 'Dual Government'.

9: Democracy Stumbles

Before the abdication of the Tsar, the revolution had been mostly confined to Petrograd, but as news of his departure spread so did the rebellion, with many pleased to be free of the Tsar, from workers, soldiers and peasants to the small middle class and even some higher up. Russia had expelled a monarchy in just a few days and a democracy was forming. Russia's Tsarist system had been so fatally undermined in the build-up to 1917 that it could not fight back and at this point there was no civil war. It was a remarkable change. All eyes were on the Provisional Government. But this fledgling democracy was crippled from the start.

Prince Lvov: Prime Minister

Prince Lvov was a gifted administrator and a man used to hard, practical work. He was one of Russia's most able men. Unfortunately, he had no experience of party politics, and Russia was now divided into a mass of competing political groups. Russia depended on him steering a way through. He was a gentleman in a government of cunning and strident politicians, a zemstvo man in a world of socialist groups, all with small dogmatic differences he did not understand. He ruled for four months with an optimism the situation did not deserve, with a naïve belief that the people of

149

Russia were good and democratic and would flock to peaceful western methods. His leadership of the Provisional Government meant trusting the people would wait for a constitutional assembly to redraw Russia, and all that was needed was a liberal, mild government some distance away from local interests to guide people there. He wanted neither force nor coercion to get Russia to follow this path and to keep this state intact. Those like him in government had grown up disliking the state and authority and would not use it on people, even when Bolsheviks threatened.

Many in Russia had their eyes on what they felt was the revolution's spiritual forefather: the success and failure of the French Revolution. Even the Bolsheviks did and saw themselves as Jacobins. The French revolution wasn't much further in time from the Russian than the latter is to us, and an awful lot of what happens next in this book occurred with people pondering what the French did.

The Flaws in Government

Unfortunately, Russia was Russia, not France, and Lvov and the PG danced round the issue of land reform, so desired by the peasants, and social reform, so desired by the workers. True, what they started with was a vast series of reforms, designed to make Russia the freest country in the world: freedom of speech, race, religion, universal suffrage, the police brought into line, the end of the death penalty, the implementation of local government.

However, there were several problems. Firstly, they made the country free by wiping away the old regime, which was easy enough for them as they had spent years in opposition to it. But they rarely replaced this with any working alternative, because they had no experience of administration, knowing only what they wanted to get rid of, not create. From dissolving the police to disliking centralized government while not instituting a working decentralized replacement, the PG was a mess. On March 5th it sacked all the governors and gave their jobs to zemstvos. The latter were far from ready, but what else could these poorly trained, liberal rebels visualise?

In addition, political changes were not what people wanted: they wanted social and land reform. Russia had a divided government, with the PG ignoring key areas and the soviet holding real power, but even the latter was divided and unwilling to use power, split into a morass of smaller groups. The soviet, with its rejection of government, police, politicians, priests and land owners, appealed to the street because it (in theory) offered class changes, the thing that had inspired people. Even then, the central soviets like Petrograd had only loose control over hundreds if not thousands of devolved local ones. But the soviet would not take power.

This failure to rebuild the state was not helped by the PG spending far too long trying to create the perfect system for electing and running the Constituent Assembly, which would have given Russia a fledging democratic parliament if they had just got on with it and created it. Could Russia have built around the Assembly? We don't know, it took too long to form. Time was wasted and events outpaced it. The central government of Russia had been washed away, a fractured new one formed, and beneath it Russia divided down into a mass of small soviets. The realm of the intellectuals was the cities, not the countryside.

Land reform and the question of the war were not obscure points identified much later by historians. Millions of Russian soldiers had fought since 1914 in a war which had literally broken the Russian government. Finding a solution should have been paramount. Land reform wasn't obscure either, as anyone who had been anywhere near the countryside would have found out very quickly, as would anyone who read the piles of petitions sent by terrified gentry to the PG asking for help. Ignoring these issues was a colossal dereliction of duty.

Peasants and Soldiers

The peasant mir was now reinvigorated as a peasant soviet (but basically a slightly evolved commune) when old patriarchal power brokers lost ground to the young and advanced peasants who had brought their land (and skills) together into soviets. Then the commune went after the gentry and larger landowners' estates as peasants organized marches on their overlords. In spring 1917 these marches aimed just to gain concessions, while waiting for the PG to solve the land question by law. In summer, the peasants stopped waiting and took the land, mostly thanks to peasant soldiers. A land revolution followed that the government could not stop. With the police broken and the army in rebellion, local government was revolutionary. The peasants then stopped looking to Petrograd and made their own law because things in the PG had taken too long. The All Russian Peasant Assembly had no legal force in the old sense, but the peasants gave it a legal force in this new world. When all the peasants signed up to one law - their ownership of all the land - what really was the law of the grey men in Petrograd? Curiously, one of the reasons why Lenin (and thus the Bolsheviks) supported the complete transfer of land to the peasants was thanks to conversations Lenin had with the exiled Father Gapon of 1905 fame.

Workers also wanted a vast amount of new rules and laws: better wages, proper food, decent working hours, and a government to put wage and good controls in place, and take over factories, to regulate it all and avoid inflation and money-grabbing employers. Foremen had to start being polite or be beaten up. Women wanted equal pay (and, correctly, equal everything). Almost all workers engaged in discussions of politics, thanks to an infant political culture, and a huge amount of trade unions, soviets and new factory committees were created. These were designed to favour the worker while also keeping production going: no one wanted everything for free as in the American media's scaremongering cartoon of socialism; they wanted to work too, but fairly. Workers feared factory owners would shut them down and starve them out, so factory committees ensured factories kept going and workers could demand their payments. A new, vastly adaptive, innovative system which leaned to demanding state control emerged in urban areas, but again the PG was slow to act. So, this new political class began to turn to the people who would act, the Bolsheviks, rather than those ponderously waiting, the PG.

Red Guards formed. The revolution had left many armed workers and armed militias. They didn't disarm, and stayed in workers brigades in industrial areas, while the government used its own militias in better-off areas. Soviets brought these workers under their banner, but Bolsheviks got into them, labelled them Red Guard and changed their direction. Young, literate, revolutionary, they leaned to Bolshevik extremism, not the soviet, certainly not the PG.

The PG declined to keep up with any of this, but as war raged, workers grew upset that the PG was not giving them more (and more) concessions, and employers grew angry, feeling too many were being given. The PG also failed to address nationalism, believing in the whole Russian geography, and confusingly giving people rights without giving them their own countries. Independence movements in the fringes soared with a different take on the peasants: socialist independents wanting the land held by 'foreign elites' given to locals. The PG gave in on Poland, which had the German army in it anyway, but not elsewhere. In Finland, the PG threatened war. In Ukraine, it offered concessions, but PG elements inflamed nationalism and triggered a constitutional crisis (which we'll return to later).

The Soviet Joins the Provisional Government

Back at the war, Order Number One meant the army was only clinging on as a fighting force, because soldiers didn't want to fight, they wanted to go home to new land and rights. They certainly weren't going to be brutalized by officers, who they had a tendency to terrify and murder. Demands expanded from 'we're not attacking the Germans' to 'we only want to be soldiers for eight hours a day'. The PG initially avoided the war question, because the people thought it was an imperial war that should be ended, but the PG

155

wondered at what cost? Russia had commitments to allies abroad. It had elements wanting to continue the war, but there was no agreement over war aims, which seemed to include both agreeing with soviet and quitting, and not letting western allies down, a stark set of opposites. A long argument over how this was possible followed. When the Foreign Minister told the allies of the soviet's plans to quit and his own plans to keep an eye on conquering Constantinople, the situation worsened and it led to battles on the street, the threat of troops fighting troops.

The PG was crumbling, Petrograd was on the verge of civil war over the international war and the soviet … well they did what they'd thought about for a while and sent people to join the PG. The people were hopeful, because the former wasn't working, and they thought the soviet would end the war and divide the land. In fact, they really wanted the soviet to take sole charge, elbowing out the PG, but the leaders of the soviet actually just wanted to quell violence. On May 2nd, to stop civil war and extremists, the soviet voted to join the PG. They took six of sixteen cabinet seats, as private citizens and not soviet members (well, only technically). This included Kerensky dealing with the war. There were no plans to offer an armistice and end it, just a socialist PG member trying to organise a conference of socialists from the warring nations to apply joint pressure for a wholesale end, which was entirely thin air and fantasy.

In reality, this union destroyed the soviet's viability along with the PG and left the door open for the extremists it was trying to stop. Bolshevism grew as the centre declined, and left and right drifted away from a / the failing government to hard liners, just like Germany in the 1930s. All the union achieved was that the soviet would be seen to fail just as much as the dithering PG.

Lenin Returns

During the February revolution, Lenin was still in exile in Zurich; he had nothing to do with it. This left him the task of getting back to Russia across war-torn Europe. The British blocked the sea and didn't want a man who campaigned for the war to end to cross it, so it had to be land. Exiled socialists formulated a plan for them to be exchanged back to Russia for German prisoners. Germany was keen, less so for the thought of their internees returning, more to cause trouble for Russia by letting Lenin loose, a major destabilising factor. As plans go, this worked perfectly. The PG was slow to agree because they also knew what problems would be caused, so Lenin and thirty-one others agreed for them, and on March 27th they left, on a supposedly sealed train (one not meant to be checked or searched en route), arriving in Petrograd on April 3rd 1917 to a welcoming committee of red-bearing soldiers, workers and people who'd come straight from a major Bolshevik conference. The station he'd turned up at was in the Vyborg district, an industrial heartland. But was he really home?

Lenin had spent seventeen years in exile, barring six months in the 1905 revolution, and was behind on the state of Russia, spending most of his adult life as a professional revolutionary. Perhaps this is how he could become a cold dictator, because he had been split apart from the people he would control and had little understanding or empathy with them. Even now he was planning a new, second revolution, which he would lead, and in *Letters From Afar* he'd planned it: a Bolshevik breach with the PG, then with the Mensheviks, then arm workers, have the Bolsheviks take power and end the war. These ideas were turned into his ten-point April Theses, delivered when his train arrived. His return saw a public speech and the next day he was lecturing socialists in the Tauride Palace, amazing and horrifying them at the same time. Gone was the previous and widespread socialist belief in the bourgeois revolution of the middle class, instead Lenin called for an immediate revolution and power to workers and peasants. This was extreme stuff, further left than the vast majority of even Bolsheviks. Lenin had no dates for the revolution, just a plan to begin gathering support. Indeed, he was jeered by the left and Lvov was informed Lenin had lost the plot. Most Bolsheviks in Petrograd had been supporting the PG and working with the other socialists, even considering reunification with the Bolsheviks and refusing to print any more of Lenin's Letters From Afar as they seemed totally divorced from reality. They thought this was the time to come together. Lenin had the exact opposite view.

But Lenin was a belligerent genius whose violent language found a home in a chaotic situation. There was no Lenin outside politics, and 1917 was all he had ever worked for. He was desperate to win. Unfortunately, he was cold and unfeeling with it, a trait desired by revolutionaries ever since Chernyshevsky's novel *What Is To Be Done* popularised a protagonist who was both hell bent on revolution and utterly heartless and inhumane. Lenin was prepared to shed other people's blood, a cold political machine who didn't care what others thought and who opposed any disagreement with him. He was willing to smash anything in Russia to take power. In a terrible way, this gave him an edge when everyone else held back for fear of damage.

Lenin now tried to remake the Bolsheviks into an obedient party doing what he wanted and that alone. It would take a while, it would be a struggle, but in contrast the Mensheviks (who failed at all this) didn't even have a single obvious leader. Although Lenin wasn't successful in the sense that the Bolsheviks were still riven by faction, he was in the

159

sense that he rode the rank and file to ultimate power. The entire Bolshevik Party in Petrograd was moving to reconciliation with the rest of the socialists before Lenin arrived and made them pivot 180 degrees, not because of deep-seated policy or even pseudo-science Marxism, but because that was what one man, Lenin, demanded. The Germans were delighted.

Changing the Situation

Some right-leaning Bolsheviks went to the Mensheviks, lessening internal opposition, but the centre of the party was pulled into Lenin's orbit by a reduction in the extremes of his ideas: a carefully pitched change, removing the immediate revolution against the PG. However a large number of left-wing Bolsheviks had been drawn in by calls for immediate action and asked why wait? In mid-April one Bolshevik faction tried a coup and failed, during which Lenin stayed quiet and distant. This was Lenin's problem: he had to wait until the Bolsheviks had a mass of support or else a revolution would fail, but if he waited too long he might lose control of his extreme militants. Lenin needed to harness a force of nature. Another example was the Kronstadt sailors, who declared their own Soviet Republic under local Bolsheviks. Lenin rejected this too, but tried to keep their armed threat on side. A negotiated peace between the sailors and the PG left the former as a sword of Damocles hanging over the PG's heads, a sword which wanted Lenin to get on with things.

In June, the 'Military Organization' of the Petrograd armed forces (run by Bolsheviks), boosted by ever-more Bolshevik soldiers, planned an armed march to show their power, and Bolshevik leaders found themselves asked to support it or lose the soldiers. But while the troops thought the political situation was right for revolution, and as strikes among workers pushed the tensions to explosive levels, Lenin banned the march: they did not feel able to win yet.

Lenin called for revolution, but was not yet willing to lead it when people below him started one. When the Soviet called for a peaceful demonstration, the Bolsheviks were able to dominate it. But it changed nothing.

It is worth pointing out an opposition to the above view. For Richard Pipes, the April demonstration wasn't just a failed Bolshevik armed-seizure of power, but one of a series of failed attempts Lenin made until he succeeded in October 1917. June saw Lenin order an attempt at a coup and fail to gain enough support. He ducked early, and the soviet declined to crush him in punishment. For Pipes, the history of 1917 is a new democracy being constantly assailed by Lenin. This book, however, argues that there were more factors at play and Lenin's role in 1917 was murkier and less binary. It argues

161

that in Petrograd there were large social currents which people at various times tried to harness, and which in the end Lenin rode to a dictatorship that he was able to make last through civil war. Ultimately, he was the only leader of 1917 willing to destroy everything in Russia, to wage a bloody civil war in order to secure his own power. It just took him a few attempts to either find the nerve to stand up and try or judge the moment right.

CRIB

- The Provisional Government and the Soviet shared power, one with liberal/legal legitimacy and one representing the masses of Russia.

- However, both the PG and the Soviet avoided the two key questions: how to solve the land and World War One problems.

- The peasants of Russia socialized and pushed forward land 'reform', actually theft. The workers swiftly evolved a new (socialist) political culture, demanding rights and powers.

- With Petrograd on the verge of civil strife over the war, the soviet and PG joined forces. Now both would be blamed for all the failures and avoiding the war and land questions.

- Lenin, a revolutionary who wanted an armed coup and his own Bolshevik power, was allowed back to Russia by Germany to cause trouble.

- However, Lenin kept turning down chances to try his coup.

10: The War Destroys

The War and the Attack

The combined Provisional Government wanted to continue their part in World War One. Why? They thought they had to in order to keep Russia intact, because any negotiation or surrender to Germany and Austria-Hungary would involve huge loss of land and resources. No one wanted to oversee the breakdown of a Russian Empire they all thought should remain. In addition, the acceptance of the PG by Britain and France depended on the former maintaining their role in a war the latter still very much wanted to win. That was the base level. Some in the PG looked higher than this, believing that Russia's war aims (which included conquering Constantinople) were still on the cards, and rather than break up under revolution the Russian map could grow. Others feared that a surrender, or even some form of agreed peace, would play into the hands of extreme socialists.

You might be thinking, how could anyone in the PG have looked at how the war was going and think things would improve? We turn to the French Revolution. The PG felt the army would be energized by revolutionary fervour and a newly born and free populace would rush to the front and attack to defend their new rights and prove as successful as when the French Revolutionary Wars exported revolution across Europe.

Kerensky, who will feature heavily now, had been made Minister for War and he appointed Brusilov as Commander in Chief of the army. The latter was the most successful Russian general and a man who supported the revolution. Brusilov was a pragmatist, and he was willing to work with soldiers' committees because he believed only reform could lead to victory. Under the Tsar, Brusilov had come to the conclusion that if he could save either Russia or the Tsar he would save the former. He'd do what was needed. He wasn't buying into taking the Ottoman capital, but he supported the desire of Russia's western allies for a 1917 offensive to try and win the war together. He thought Russia must decide the time and place of the next major battle by attacking first rather than leave the choice to the Germans. In reality Germany was planning on leaving the east on the defensive, and no attack could have been better than what happened. Indeed, Brusilov was trapped between two poles. His support for the socialist soldiers meant the upper echelon of officers disliked him, while his faith in those soldiers meant he thought they would fight and win, when they weren't keen on the former and had little interest in the latter if their farms and cities were miles away. Brusilov burned his support from the soldiers by asking for an offensive, and the anti-war Bolsheviks gained.

As the attack came closer, Kerensky loved the fact he was being portrayed as a hero. Indeed, he liked it so much he started to believe it. The PG encouraged it, Kerensky did tours of the soldiers, whom he thought were people wanting to fight. He was the sort of person who wore a military uniform even though he wasn't in the military. Brusilov, to his credit, realized there was a problem, and that soldiers turning to Bolshevism wanted to end the war and were deserting in large numbers. He also knew they weren't Bolshevik because of socialist theory, but because that was the group who wanted to end the war. He then realized the attack was going to fail. But at this point Brusilov also realized it didn't matter what he reported or ordered; Kerensky was running the army and the attack would begin regardless because he had a delusion and a reputation to maintain.

Failure and Resignation

Bombardment began on June 16th, and on the 18th troops attacked. They made initial progress and looked like a success, before the soldiers at the front felt they had done enough and the ones behind them wouldn't take their place. The advance stopped, fell apart and was counter attacked; the offensive had failed. It cost four hundred thousand casualties and miles of land. The anti-war Bolsheviks now became the soldiers' firm favourites. You do not have to be a political expert to see why, and if the PG had ended the war instead of fighting it there might have been no Bolshevik revolution.

Everyone associated with the attack was in trouble, chief of all the PG. As recrimination began, the PG splintered. On July 2nd three ministers resigned over issues in Ukraine, but it was the war that caused the sundering. Land and war issues were still unsolved, the latter going hideously wrong. As the left moved hard-left and the right moved hard-right, the coalition in the PG was lost and on July 3rd Lvov resigned. He thought only civil war and slaughter would follow. The offensive had been a turning point.

Another Bolshevik Failure

The Bolsheviks had been building power. They had troops in the capital, the ten thousand men of the elite First Machine Gun Regiment among them. The Bolsheviks dominated industrial areas. Then the PG did something ill advised. The soldiers in the capital had been kept away from the war as the troops felt they had made the revolution and would defend it, so had demanded to stay local. Sending them off to fight was seen as a threat to the revolution, a way of subverting socialist demands. Yet, on June 20th, the machine gunners were ordered to the front to attack for exactly that

167

reason: Kerensky and others wanted to use the war to free the PG of Petrograd's troops. They even considered moving the capital to Moscow instead to make their lives easier. The Machine Gunners reacted with fury and planned an uprising. Word spread, the army prepared and the Bolshevik Military Organization became the central organiser. But ... Lenin and Bolshevik central command were not sure and said no rebellion. As ever, Lenin and company doubted while others below them were ready to take action. Lenin said the Bolsheviks were not ready and needed more power in the soviet and in Russia or it would fail.

Lenin was, in this instance, ignored, fleeing to Finland to escape arrest by the PG. On July 4th troops started a rebellion led by low ranking Bolshevik soldiers. Workers joined them, a violent mass of people with no clear leadership. A force with no head. They marched to the site of the PG and Soviet, but no one knew what to do once they were there. Night fell, people dispersed. Bolshevik central command, minus Lenin, debated what to do: it seemed time to do something, and they sent for Lenin. There is debate whether this was a coup planned by Lenin that went wrong and which he successfully distanced himself from, but really it seems to have been a lower level uprising that the Bolshevik leaders once more failed to harness. They sat worrying instead, reacting ad hoc. When Lenin returned he could not decide whether to gamble or hold.

The next day the crowd came again. Lenin was still no leader. When twenty thousand Kronstadt sailors arrived, they marched to Lenin for orders: he had none. Tens of thousands of armed people were ready to be told what to do, and the Bolsheviks could have taken the PG, the Soviet and power because there was almost no one defending it. They weren't told. Lenin ducked. A mob arrested a politician, Trotsky came out and used a speech to rescue him, but did not call for power. The chance was gone and the mob fell apart. Troops loyal to the soviet then arrived, and the anti-Bolshevik counter began with the government, claiming Lenin was working with the Germans. (Intriguingly, some historians believe Lenin was being paid vast sums by the Germans, but the PG botched releasing this information in a manner which would permanently doom Lenin. For other historians, the poor release of information was because the evidence wasn't enough, i.e. he wasn't being paid.) Leaders were arrested and Lenin went into hiding again. Anti-Bolshevik movements roared into bloody life: eight hundred higher ranking Bolsheviks were captured.

However, the soviet and the other socialists did not turn on the Bolsheviks, instead moving to reduce these right-wing attacks in case they spread to all socialists, and in doing so they saved Bolshevism from extinction. The Bolsheviks would go on to extinguish the socialists instead. Yet, still, the soviet refused to take power. A coalition government was to be tried again, but this new PG didn't try to put Lenin and his fellows on trial to keep the socialists—and their quaint view of the socialist movement as a friendly close-knit scene—on side.

What had happened here? Richard Pipes is adamant that this was a planned Bolshevik coup, and perhaps this is the most uncertain event in 1917 when it comes to our conclusions. But here's the key thing: if this was a planned Bolshevik coup, then it worked. The city was theirs, they could have taken power. Even Pipes admits he doesn't know why they didn't take power, why they halted, why Lenin, a man all about struggle and violent takeover, stopped. In the planned coup version, Lenin has to lose his nerve, a streak of cowardice showing. In this book, the coup didn't occur because it wasn't a planned attempt by Lenin, but the actions of people lower down which cascaded upwards and which Lenin shied from. He had always disliked spontaneity and wasn't sure he'd win.

Kerensky in Power, Kornilov Arrives

But who to head the coalition? Kerensky was made Prime Minister by the resigning Lvov, partly because Kerensky claimed to have saved the front line. Lvov went to a monastery and then exile abroad. Kerensky was the only man left with support in the left, the liberals and the military, and he was also developing into an egomaniac who slept in the Tsar's bed and thought himself the saviour of the nation. The scene was not set for great success. The new PG, led by Kerensky, turned away from the streets and the demands of the soviet. Even the soviet's representatives on the PG, who still sat as civilian politicians, were on the right of that spectrum, and the soviet itself was so reduced it was even thrown out of the building and sent to a former school called the Smolny Institute. Freedoms were curbed. Had Kerensky ended the war, he might have lived up to his dream. He didn't.

Russia was becoming a country of extremes. The army was retreating, mobs were killing people, hopes of a new era were gone and demands for force to be used spread. The rich lived hedonistically before they were killed, right-wing groups attacked socialists on the streets. With the extreme left looking to the Bolsheviks, the extreme right pushed forward. When Brusilov refused to entertain either Kerensky or himself as dictator Kerensky sacked him, which pleased many of the military elites, and replaced him with General Kornilov, a right-wing hard liner considered a potential saviour of the rich. Kornilov became a focus of the right opposition, despite humble origins himself.

Kerensky planned to become dictator and needed a military strongman. Kornilov may have planned the same with a political strongman in Kerensky. Kornilov presented Kerensky with a list of 'reforms' which would have created a right-wing government, if not an actual dictatorship, such as the death penalty for workers' meetings. Kornilov thought he was saving the PG from socialism, rather than staging a coup against the PG, but was the sort of man who thought fighting WWI until Russia won was a good idea. Kerensky, who wanted to be in charge, would claim that Kornilov was planning a coup to erase both him and the PG, and Kornilov was being urged to do exactly that. Two rivals, one leaning to the left, one on the right. Kerensky and Kornilov orbited each other over the reforms, the former unwilling and unable to pass them through the soviet, the latter convinced executions could save Russia's fighting ability. Kornilov positioned troops, thinking he had permission from Kerensky to be ready to crush Bolsheviks, soviets and Petrograd's garrison in the event of a rebellion.

Kerensky was still undecided, wanting to be the man who allied left and right. However, most turned against him for not being left or right enough. Kerensky could not decide to go either way, for if he went right he'd lose the socialists, but if he went left Kornilov would attack. So Kerensky called a conference ... but in a piece of naked cowardice, it was in

Moscow. With the aim of uniting support, it just showed the divide between workers and the middle class, and Kerensky's attempts to dominate the conference failed when Kornilov arrived, where the right treated him like a hero, raising him to their shoulders. Kerensky had now lost them, and quit the conference. He knew he had failed, he thought Kornilov would start a coup. In truth, while Kornilov was the sort of man who thought the military should sort out the government, he accepted Kerensky as that government. It was the soviet Kornilov didn't like.

The Kornilov Affair

Then something strange happened. Something so strange you couldn't use it in fiction. Vladimir Lvov (right-winger, madman, sacked Procurator of the Holy Synod) inserted himself between Kornilov and Kerensky as a mediator. Lvov told Kerensky that Kornilov was planning to have him killed. Kerensky sent Lvov to find out the details. Lvov then appeared to Kornilov, pretending to be an emissary from Kerensky. No one asked for official papers, and Lvov offered a deal from Kerensky, when he actually had nothing: choose a Kerensky dictatorship, a Kornilov dictatorship aided by Kerensky, or a collective one.

Kornilov believed this to be real. He said he'd prefer his own but would aid a Kerensky one and invited him to

173

discuss it. Lvov then went to Kerensky, and said Kornilov demanded to be a dictator, giving a three-point ultimatum: Petrograd under martial law, a new cabinet to be picked by Kornilov, and all power to him. Kerensky didn't bother to check if this was true, he was too busy using it as a reason to destroy his rival. Kerensky began a conversation with Kornilov on a piece of young telecoms technology, and the two spoke at total cross-purposes (the tapes of this exchange exist and transcripts are available). It would be funny if people hadn't been killed because of it.

Kerensky announced Kornilov was planning a dictatorship, presented it to the PG, who made him an effective dictator instead. Kornilov was told he was sacked via a telegram and thought Kerensky was now a Bolshevik prisoner, as it was all so strange and confused. Kornilov thus ordered a march to free him, and the PG, from the Bolsheviks. Kornilov's troops approached Petrograd. One clear sign that Kornilov was caught up in a charade and not coldly trying his own coup at this point was that he stayed behind; when it came to physical courage he was the opposite of Lenin. Kerensky claimed this was treason (it wasn't yet), sacked him for rebelling and tried to destroy him. When Kornilov realized he finally did rebel. What other options did he have left?

The soviet, previously opposed to Kerensky as dictator, now supported him rather than have Kornilov march in.

Soviets called Kornilov the counterrevolution. Also, they formed a new counter-counter revolutionary committee, and such was the fear of the right that the Bolsheviks were forgiven and invited onto it. Kerensky had to beg for help, releasing socialist leaders and arming the workers, which meant Bolsheviks were let out of prison and smoothly took charge of the military situation as Red Guards formed under their command. Now workers and soldiers were armed and ready to repel the attack. No other leading military commander joined Kornilov, and as soon as his marching army realized it was all a confused mess, they quit. But things got worse.

Kornilov was still around the apparatus of controlling the military. Kerensky had sacked him, but for a few days he couldn't find anyone willing to go and relieve command and there was still a world war raging, so Kerensky had to order the military to follow Kornilov's orders despite him technically being in the middle of treason. It was a pathetic showing, and gives you some insight into how a load of Bolsheviks could persuade people they actually had an alternative to this horror show.

Kornilov considered suicide, but his wife talked him out of it. He was arrested but would later escape. The Kornilov Revolt had failed bloodlessly, and this time it really was bloodlessly.

CRIB

- The Russian government, both PG and socialist alike, decide a major offensive is the best way to tackle the war problem.

- Minister for War, Kerensky, organises the attack and starts to consider himself the future saviour of the nation.

- Just before the attack, even the ludicrously optimistic General Brusilov realises the soldiers won't fight.

- The attack starts and goes well for a few hours, stalls, then fails completely.

- Brusilov resigns, and Lenin refuses yet another chance to stage an armed revolt. His Bolsheviks are repressed.

- Kerensky becomes Prime Minister, and appoints General Kornilov.

- Kerensky and Kornilov become involved in a power struggle, the 'Kornilov Affair' fails as Kornilov's troops will not crush revolution in the capital.

- In repelling the Kornilov advance, the Bolsheviks have been rehabilitated and are swiftly gaining practical power.

- Kerensky is left politically crippled.

11: The October Revolution

Kornilov was arrested, Kerensky had won. Except he hadn't. The right had been angered by the betrayal of Kornilov and turned away from Kerensky. The left had been Bolshevized and suspected Kerensky of having no loyalty to the left and a secret agenda of counterrevolutionaries in his own faction. Left and right fought and soldiers quit in such numbers the army ceased to be a fighting force. Workers had weapons, and along with the soldiers they looked to Lenin and the Bolsheviks as the only people who would act. Kerensky created a five-man Directory, as in the French Revolution, to lead. It was ignored, and people expected the Bolsheviks to take power. Little could be done to resist, such was the paralysis. Even Kerensky was crumbling, heavily using drugs.

The Bolsheviks were now gaining more members in factories, soviets, the army and local government. From around ten thousand members in April 1917, a position on the side-lines of Russian politics if not the wilderness, the party reached half a million in October. For the first time they had a large party supporting them, with an entire political culture among the working class turning to them and electing them to the soviets and factory committees instead of other socialists. The Bolsheviks, with their call for peace and power to the soviet, were preferred. They alone looked untouched by the failure of 1917. Liberals, Mensheviks, SR socialists, the PG, all damned in the eyes of too many. Trotsky, now a Bolshevik, took over the Petrograd Soviet and brought with him a team of expert revolutionaries who would help. It was Trotsky who spoke as Lenin hid and schemed.

Lenin Agitates

But it was not exactly the Bolsheviks that people wanted in charge. They did not demand a Lenin dictatorship, which is what they got; they wanted a soviet government which would work for the benefit of workers and peasants, allowing soldiers to go back to being either. It just so happened the Bolsheviks were the only people arguing for the soviet to take power, and to end the war. The Bolsheviks had to call for power to soviets run by them, not a government of just Bolsheviks. The Bolshevik lie was that the October Revolution would be the soviet seizure of power with a Bolshevik agenda. In reality it was just Lenin and his team seizing power under that veil. People wanted Bolsheviks running soviets, not Lenin as emperor. The numbers of people who voted were falling, as they were growing tired of being asked to when nothing seemed to happen. As the Bolshevik vote increased the numbers of votes overall shrank, increasing the Bolshevik percentages.

The PG was paralysed, the other socialists declining. Strikes paralysed the city, violence spread. People called for the economy to be taken over to feed people and pay them. Peasants, angry at the indecision, went to take land for themselves. Communes organized land grabs and the countryside burned. Often the rich did too. Russia seemed to be descending into anarchy, with violence everywhere and calls for different forms of government.

The rest of the socialists pondered a socialist coalition to use the soviet to take power and install a socialist democracy. Lenin, wanting his own Bolshevik revolution but still doubting, joined in. Lenin offered that if socialists would take power using the soviet, he would ally with them and end his plans for an armed uprising. They had a choice, and the Democratic Conference was held to discuss whether the soviet should form a combined socialist government without the OG and Duma hangovers. It was a poorly thought-out disaster riven by faction. An emergency session decided to side with the Kadets in a coalition PG under Kerensky to last until the November elections to the Constituent Assembly, whose corpse was being dug up again. The soviet had told Lenin no. They missed a chance for the future and non-Bolshevik socialist support collapsed. The other socialists did not know what was happening around them and let themselves become irrelevant.

The socialists had many clever people, but not many politicians, or people capable of leading. Soon, one would step forward and take power for himself: Lenin. With the soviet coalition gone, Lenin began his campaign for the armed seizure of power now that he felt he had the support. He must take this power before the Constituent Assembly created a new government, and before Petrograd fell to the Germans. He did this in a letter campaign from outside Petrograd, absent because he was afraid of being arrested himself. Lenin demanded his people seize arms and revolt; it was finally the time and the situation was ripe. The Bolshevik leaders still in the city tried to ignore him and steer peacefully until the Soviet Congress on October 20th, using this to declare power. Trotsky agreed with using the meeting. Lenin raged.

Why the difference? The Bolsheviks were gaining power in the soviets all the time, and local dumas too as people turned away from the failed Mensheviks and other moderates. Surely if the Bolsheviks just waited and used the Congress as cover to take power they would win? Well, here's the thing: if the Congress of Soviets took power there would be a coalition of socialists, and Bolsheviks who weren't Lenin would end up as powerful as Lenin. If the Bolsheviks seized power, Lenin would rule undisputed and peaceful members would be out in the cold. Then Lenin could use the congress to rubber stamp what he'd done. Lenin knew this would bring civil war, and welcomed its cleansing capabilities, as he had a startling lack of empathy. It's often said that it's easier to beg for forgiveness than to ask permission, and it is easier still when you have just seized power. To doubly make sure of this, Lenin's people fudged the rules of the congress to make sure it had a disproportionately high number of Bolshevik representatives. There was also pressure to take power, in whatever way, before voting for the Constituent Assembly took place and a new veneer of legal government appeared on things to block Lenin's way.

Lenin returned to Petrograd to get things moving. On October 20th, a minority of the Bolshevik Central Committee met, chaired by Lenin (who was still hiding). He made them pass a vote to have an armed rebellion, meaning Lenin had staged a coup of his own party, and could now stage one in Russia. Without Lenin doing this, the Bolsheviks would have ended up in a soviet coalition. It meant finally, after several clear and easy opportunities, Lenin had decided to go for it.

The soviet was settling into the Smolny Institute. It was filled with soldiers protecting it, and meetings were held in a ballroom, with other rooms used by smaller committees. The Bolshevik central committee was in room 36. Other Bolsheviks were now thinking of maybe armed rebellion in a year. People on the street seemed to be hesitant of another failure. Lenin first tried to use the North Regional Congress of

Soviets to declare itself and march on Petrograd, but it demurred. Meetings of the Bolshevik Military Organization, factory committees, unions, soviets and others all told Lenin people needed time and were scared, that it would take something major for them to act. This was not the time for an uprising. Lenin disagreed, believing he only needed a small army to stage first a coup and then a fait accompli to the soviet and the people. Lenin won the argument. This was his drive. Lenin and the people on the street had swapped places.

There was still a World War on, and Germany seemed to be planning an attack on the Russian capital, Petrograd. Kerensky's answer to this was first to suggest moving the capital to Moscow, but he dropped the plan when the soviet informed him they suspected him of undermining the revolution. He then planned for how to deal with the German attack. The soviet decided to allow the Military Revolutionary Committee to organise Petrograd's defences, which was a problem as the Bolsheviks pretty much ran it. Lenin had his own army disguised as the soviet in the MRC, and a rubber stamp disguised as the soviet in the Congress, if he could only use them properly.

A Revolution Starts Without Lenin

Bolshevik sub-leader Kamenev had had enough. He resigned from the BCC to publish an essay against Lenin's plan in a newspaper, revealing it to the nation. Suddenly, the rumours were confirmed. Lenin reacted by demanding Kamenev be thrown out of the party. The Soviet Congress was pushed back to October 25th to give time for non-Bolshevik support to gather. Although opposed to Bolsheviks, non-Bolsheviks refused to act to stamp out the rebellion out of misplaced brotherhood. But while the people would not rise for Lenin at this point, they would rise if the soviet was in danger. Remarkably, Kerensky then managed to push the PG into putting the soviet in danger. Kerensky had retreated into a 'last Tsar' style land of fantasy about his power and popularity, of which he had little. Plenty of people disliked the Bolsheviks, but few wanted to crush them if it meant having to support Kerensky. On the right, monarchists thought a failed Bolshevik revolution would allow the monarchy to return, so wanted to give them the chance.

Kerensky mixed all this together and believed he could defeat a Bolshevik uprising, and he wanted the opportunity. Rather than arrest the Bolshevik leaders or attack Smolney, he ordered the Petrograd garrison be moved to the front. This managed to both look counter to the whole revolution while upsetting swathes of the capital. He thought he would trigger a Bolshevik grab at power, smash it and finish with a tame garrison. He was utterly wrong. This looked like an attack on the soviet, and the Military Revolutionary Committee formed to organise defence against Kerensky. But it was led by Trotsky and was a Bolshevik puppet. The Bolsheviks could now pretend they were defending the soviet, that any revolt would be for the soviet, even though Bolsheviks were really behind it. When the Petrograd garrison reacted with mutiny, they signed up to the MRC.

On October 21st, the MRC declared itself in charge of the Petrograd garrison, and sent commissars to command troops; they were welcomed. By October 23rd the MRC had gained control of artillery pointed at key buildings. The PG had lost military control of the city, as Kerensky found he could not call in the military to crush Bolshevism without risking being swept away himself by right-wingers still angry over the treatment of Kornilov. The October Revolution happened on the 25th, but the city was really taken on the 23rd because this wouldn't be a Bolshevik seizure of power without lots of pointless messing about before anything happened.

Lenin Seizes Power

Most Bolshevik leaders were not prepared to actually seize power, even though the door was open. They wanted the soviet congress to do it on the 25th. They paused and pondered, and Trotsky even declared that an armed seizure wasn't on the table before the congress. Why rush it? If they went and failed, the Bolsheviks would be isolated, whereas in a few hours they

185

could use the soviet. Legitimacy seemed guaranteed if they waited. Indeed, Bolshevik leaders (who weren't Lenin) were trying to gain enough votes for a soviet takeover of power, with a union of socialists in power.

It was the people who had moved. MRC forces seized ever-more control of the city: railways, banks, barracks etc. The Red Guard had replaced the police. Lower ranking Bolsheviks took power. Suddenly, people became afraid of another July, when the to seize power had been chance. At this point, Lenin acted decisively. He travelled to Smolny in disguise, only just avoiding arrest, and bullied the Bolshevik Central Committee into starting the seizure of power. The order was given: insurrection. A new Bolshevik government was drawn up, led by 'People's Commissars', a title stolen from the French Revolution because 'Minister' was considered too close to the PG. Now the Bolshevik command took control of what had happened on the streets.

This was not a vast, bloody revolution—yet. It was almost a special forces action marked by moments of comic incompetence, the collapse of a tired, bankrupt government by a few dedicated rebels using the cover of chaos on the street. The home of government, the bastion of the ministers of the PG, had almost no guards who wanted to fight. The failure to seize it quickly before the soviet congress did / could drew Lenin into a fury. Kerensky had fled to find troops, perhaps already realising he'd misjudged pretty much everything. A stronger defence could have repelled this coup.

The Bolshevik dominated MRC gave the PG and the palace an ultimatum: surrender, or a cruiser anchored nearby would blow it to pieces. The PG refused, believing the Bolsheviks had no support, and at 9.40pm the *Aurora* fired a blank. Then real fire began (but not at the palace). At 10.40pm, the long-awaited soviet congress began. The Bolsheviks did not have an absolute majority. Proceedings went on, people called for a democratic united socialist government to avoid civil war, and a motion passed. Then...

Then the Mensheviks and SRs complained about the Bolsheviks attacking the PG and walked out in protest to their doom. The Bolshevik moderates who defied Lenin and looked for consensus were undermined, leaving Lenin and his remaining soviet sympathisers to control it. They could use it to declare a Bolshevik government under a soviet flag. Lenin's plan had entirely worked, and moderate socialism had committed suicide by walking out. The Mensheviks and SRs were deemed traitors. The Winter Palace then fell and the members of the PG, except Kerensky, were locked up. Soviet power was declared, but this was not February, this was not the mass of Petrograd on the streets, this was not even August—this was a Bolshevik coup. Once more socialists had allowed the Bolsheviks the upper hand by stupidly walking out and not fighting, as if this was some child's debating society and not the fate of millions of people at stake. This time, however, that stupidity was terminal. As they left, Trotsky summed up the situation perfectly; they went "into the dustbin of history". When Lenin arrived at the congress, having taken the Russian capital, he brought decrees he had written on the land and on the war. He tackled the key issues that had destroyed democracy on his first day.

Kerensky was outside Petrograd trying to gather loyal troops. Many generals were reluctant to help either in case their forces mutinied, because they hated the man, or, in the case of the Cossack Third Cavalry, because their commander had killed himself over the Kornilov affair and they blamed Kerensky. There were other problems, like the railway union demanding the Bolsheviks form a government with other socialists, and they were too powerful to completely ignore because the railways could either move or block PG troops. Many in Bolshevik high command thought they could only survive by allying with these groups, but the other socialists demanded Lenin be kept from ultimate command, and Lenin flatly refused. Even when five of the Bolshevik central committee quit over censorship (the straw that broke their backs), he threatened to keep ruling by calling in the sailors and refusing to limit himself. The rebels conceded the point.

Moscow was a scene of civil war as Bolsheviks struggled to take power there. The liberals finally found a force to move towards Petrograd. To get the railway loyalty, the Bolsheviks agreed to a form of cross-party talks (weighted in favour of them and with no lessening of Lenin's power). However, the Mensheviks and other socialists demanded a full surrender of the October revolution and the return of a coalition government with no Lenin. As you can imagine, that completely overplayed their hand and they lost support when the counter-revolutionary army folded and violence in Moscow went the Bolsheviks' way. This allowed Lenin to sneer at talks with other socialists and they failed. He had taken power, so now he attacked the members of the Bolshevik party who had been opposed, purging the central committee and facing the task of running a Russia that had defeated several previous governments.

Few people thought the Bolsheviks would last (including many Bolsheviks). Quite a few didn't even realise it was now Bolsheviks in charge and not, finally, the soviet. Across the cities of the Russian heartland, Bolsheviks took control in any number of subtle variations. On the fringes, however, they were not so successful. Civil war would begin instead, and Lenin was not upset.

CRIB

- As the only people advocating an end to war, land reform and soviet power, the Bolsheviks are now very popular among the workers and soldiers.

- Lenin decides now is the time to seize power, but the streets are unsure.

- Kamenev, a Bolshevik trying to stop a coup, accidentally pushes Kerensky into an attack on the Bolsheviks which triggers the streets into starting a coup.

- Lenin manages to take charge of the rebellion, the Bolshevized troops have control of the city, and he seizes power.

- The soviet is used to add a veneer of justification, as it supports Lenin when opposition parties walk out.

12: Lenin Secures Power

The Bolsheviks had taken power, but only in a part of Russia. I don't just mean a geographic part, although they were concentrated in the heartland of old Russia. I they divided all sorts of groups. They held power amongst some classes in Petrograd, in some parts of the army, in some parts of the soviet. They notionally held power on behalf of a soviet and were supposed to fit in with a Constituent Assembly being voted on shortly after.

Indeed, the Bolshevik rule of Russia had a bad start: virtually all the organs of government (liberals and monarchists) had people who opposed the seizure and refused to work for it. This mass middle-class strike formed a group with another long name: The Committee for the Salvation of the Fatherland and the Revolution. Banks had to be robbed to get money to make the Bolshevik state work. Very few Bolsheviks knew how to run a country, or get people fed and supported. They were helped, however, by their enemies simply waiting for the collapse and not getting armed forces to crush them, and by the civil war at this point being concentrated in / fought by smaller forces on the fringes of the country rather than larger 'White' armies which would come later. The Bolsheviks were accidentally given time to consolidate and they managed it. This is how.

Lenin and Government

Lenin improvised. All top-level government was centralized in Bolshevik hands, and the rest destroyed. All lower level government was decentralized into soviets, committees and factory organizations which trended to being Bolsheviks anyway. Peasants suddenly had power to attack noble landowners, and they rejected the need for a new constituent assembly since Lenin seemed to be doing fine. Workers had responsibility for the economy, where they had to solve problems or share in the blame. Lenin centralized and shattered, establishing Bolshevik rule in the key areas, aiming to break local power at his leisure once he was secure. Plenty of old fashioned officials were retained if they agreed to work. Gaps were filled by Bolsheviks promoted to new positions and work cultures alien to them. Slowly the 'People's Commissars' gained control and their ruling unit 'Sovnarkom' (The Council of People's Commissars) took power. Lenin ran Sovnarkom as he had the party; both party and country began merging into one.

The system that came into being in Russia has been called a one-party state and a dual state. This is because the ruling party remained in being, and it was the heads of this party who took on all the roles of a government system which existed at the same time. The party leaders were the country's

192

leaders, and you had to rise through the party to get to them. There were no God-given kings, no freely elected prime ministers in charge of the nation. There were just the heads of the party, holding onto the reins of the country but pretending to be a cross-socialist soviet. If it sounds weird, it was almost unique in history (unless you count a foetal version in Jacobin France) but went on to spread over the globe, because people aren't often very original. The party had to insert its members into the civilian government in order to control this, and as the Bolsheviks spread their control across Russia, so party membership swelled in order to have an unofficial government which could keep track of the much larger official government. A dual state indeed.

Improvised, cunning, sneaky, in 1917 Sovnarkom was not an organ of state but a body of people not yet free of revolutionary dreams and one that had to pretend to be so much more than one party in charge. Lenin worked to undercut the soviet which was notionally in charge and had a tiny amount of non-Bolsheviks still left in it who could cause problems. Lenin thus allowed soviet membership to swell with Bolsheviks until it was too big to govern, and so reduced its power with that justification, while doing the opposite to Sovnarkom. Having done this Lenin side-stepped the soviet with some pseudo-legal sleights of hand and established a Russia where the leader, him, could rule by decree. (However,

Lenin tended to let those he'd appointed beneath him write and send the decrees themselves, with him just checking a few.) The Soviet was practically dead. All power to the soviets had died in days.

The SRs now divided in anger and those on the left offered to work with the Bolsheviks, even being offered some seats without any power in government so Lenin could still pretend this was a union of socialists and not a coup. In return, Lenin gave these 'Left SRs' the pleasure of allowing the Assembly to meet, and several other concessions, while he used them as sheep's clothing to pack the Peasant's Congress (still a core of SR power) with pro-Leninists,. When that failed used the Left SRs as cover to smash the Peasant's Congress, cripple the right SRs and bring the peasants' units under his control. Lenin approved peasant land seizures and gained wide support. The old system was seen to be broken, and the people were involved in a new system. No longer would the PG stand atop, a survival of the old and widely blamed, but the Bolsheviks would create something that felt new even as they destroyed and terrorized old elites and middle classes. The PG was broken, the Soviet was broken, the Soviet's Executive Committee was broken, the Peasant's Congress was broken. Soon the Constituent Assembly would be too. Of course, when this decentralized power failed and caused chaos, Lenin would put the next part of the plan into effect by taking the power back, recentralizing around Bolsheviks who were now firmly in place. Lenin wiped away the old world, invited the people to join in the chaos, and then reasserted himself to bring control.

The Death of the Constituent Assembly

Elections for the Constituent Assembly had been scheduled to start November 12th. The seizure of power had come too late to cancel the election, even though Lenin hated it and was at odds with plenty of his party who wanted the Assembly as a veneer of legitimacy. Most opposition thought this was their hope and their future, and the Bolsheviks won only 24% of the vote, a long way behind the SRs, so Sovnarkom postponed the opening of parliament. A Union for the Defence of the Constituent Assembly formed and people marched in protest at the Bolsheviks' attempts to terrify people into obedience under the banner "All Power to the Constituent Assembly". The Bolsheviks in turn banned the Kadets, arrested their leaders and began an attack on the bourgeois. Then the Bolsheviks went after socialist opposition. A police state was created, with the MRC replaced by the Cheka (later called the KGB) in order to arrest, imprison and arrest some more of any opposition voice. A war had begun on opponents to Lenin, and moderate Bolsheviks were frozen in fear of fighting back. The Jacobin Terror of the French

Revolution is an almost universally reviled period of terror and murder, and the Bolsheviks of 1917 cited it as just cause for doing what they now did. Of course, this is Russia, so Cheka was actually short-hand for yet another very long name: All Russian Extraordinary Commission for Struggle against Counter Revolution and Sabotage.

Lenin now wanted an end to the Consistent Assembly and got a declaration passed that Russia was a Union of Soviet Republic. He also ended private property. When the Assembly opened on January 5th, Petrograd was under military law and the Union for the Defence of the Constituent Assembly had no forces to try and rise up, so they marched instead but were shot at by Bolshevik troops. This wasn't February 1917 again, it wasn't even 1905, and the demonstrators fled.

Even so, the Assembly opened for a debate on whether it should live, but the Bolsheviks made sure the first proposed legislation would have removed the ability of the Assembly to pass further legislation, and when this was rejected Lenin led the Bolsheviks in a walkout. But unlike Menshevik walkouts, here the leaving party held the edge: troops. Lenin thus convened his own meeting, ordered the Assembly to shut down and troops did so after watching the last failed gasp of democracy in Russia. It never met again as there was no army to reopen it. Russia's new government was apparent two days later with a Bolshevik-packed Third Congress of Soviets that did as Lenin told it. Why didn't the Mensheviks or the SRs rise in violent anger? Because they saw the royalists and the 'right' massing armies on the fringes of the former empire and felt the Bolsheviks were the lesser evil. They were brother and sister socialists after all, in the minds of the deluded moderate socialists who just argued and rarely kicked back. There were some assassination attempts, there were some attempts at triggering a new mass strike, march and rebellion. All fizzled out.

The peasants and the workers of Russia had their communes and soviets, and wanted peace, land and food. Few wanted a parliament, fewer wanted to fight longer for it. The Bolsheviks seemed to be people who did things, and the middle class were too weak to prevent soviets and communes creating a new Bolshevik heartland. The middle class were the ones who desired a parliament and a democracy, and they weren't enough. There was bloody fighting, and more to come, but the Bolsheviks had won in Petrograd. When Lenin passed a decree for land, which basically legitimized peasants seizing the property of the rich, he went a great way to settling the issue the peasants rebelled over and won there too. One of the great arguments of 1917, the land question, was solved, just in a manner the landed really didn't like.

Reforming Russia

The Soviet / Bolshevik / Lenin revolution now began: a massive rejection of the previous government. A tearing down of class, social hierarchy, of all authority, be it from a count or a judge or a landowner. Lenin didn't stop hunger or poverty, but he gave a psychological boost to many of the working class and peasants by letting them see the rich torn down and suffering too. The human psyche likes that, so a war against the wealthy exploded. The new language of class was simply a way of reframing the ancient human nature of hate and jealousy and it created enemies of the people. These had always existed, but not with a pretend intellectual framework and a state saying it was okay. The Bolsheviks did not need to start this war, they just allowed it and shaped it into the Red Terror. The Russian people began it. The rich were forced to work and many fled to the growing opposition on the geographic fringes, which became the White's side in the civil war, or further abroad with whatever they could carry. The legal system was utterly ruined to allow mob rule and terror, with Revolutionary Tribunals as in the French Revolution and people's courts, law by revenge and fear. Lenin simply harnessed what people had started, yet again. Peasants murdered landowners and took all their riches; soldiers butchered officers and their families; workers tore down their bosses. Blood ran. Now the Bolsheviks were at one with the mood they openly stole, levying taxes on the rich to take all

198

their wealth, taxes not only taken at the end of a gun but with hostages too.

The End of the War

Lenin had seized power in a major part thanks to everyone else's failure to deal with WWI. If he didn't deal with the war he'd fail too. There now followed one of the most ludicrous episodes in military history. Lenin declared a just and democratic peace with no annexations and indemnities—which was a problem as Germany had a different view, a functioning army and a large occupied territory. No one outside of Russia in 1917 wanted to end the whole war, because Britain and France thought they would win it with US troops, and the Germans thought they would win it in the west once troops had been brought over from the almost-won east. Germany wanted land and resources and Russia was weak. How could Russia ask for no annexations? It was fantasy.

There was also ideology. Lenin was adamant that the October Revolution would trigger a series of socialist revolts in the warring nations. Why wouldn't the soldiers revolt against the imperial conflict that was killing them? It was a good question. For Lenin it was an essential one, because he thought a world, or at least Germany's socialist revolution, was essential to allowing the backward, peasant Russian one to survive. So the end of 1917 saw Lenin trying to push

Germany into revolution to end the war. Instead of pushing a conventional peace they pushed revolution to create peace.

It soon became clear to Lenin that this might not happen. So, what to do, because being invaded and taken over by the Kaiser wasn't terribly helpful either. Some Bolsheviks argued Russia must fight a war against German invaders rather than agree a peace and end hope of Germany rebelling, and these were the sort of people who had paid absolutely no attention to the reality of 1917. They felt the international socialist revolution would happen any moment and that if it didn't, if Russia conceded now and halted the current, then Russia could not survive on its own as a socialist nation. The rest knew war would destroy them as it had the previous governments. They needed to pack Germany away and focus on retaking Russia.

Lenin, and others, thought some sort of negotiated surrender to Germany would give them time to secure power. They thought it was necessary because the Russian military wouldn't fight that war for anyone anymore. Lenin was, in this instance, absolutely right. He also decided socialism would be okay in one country for the moment, and peace was the essential thing. Peace would let him secure whatever of Russia he could keep from the Germans for himself.

First, Lenin published a Peace Decree, which called on the Great Powers fighting World War One to bring the war to a close. He knew this would be refused because Britain, France and Germany were still too caught up in their imperial conflict to step back willingly. That gave Lenin some rarely earned moral high ground, but failed to stir the citizens of the Great Powers to finally take charge of their own destiny and demand the war ended.

On November 15th, Trotsky, in charge of Foreign Affairs, offered an armistice to the Germans so peace could be discussed. This was probably one of the happiest days Germany had in the war and the site of the German Eastern Front HQ, Brest-Litovsk, was picked for talks. At first Russia pushed for a general armistice, but then conceded just an eastern front one. Trotsky asked for six months' worth of talks so he could drag things out as long as possible in case of a German rebellion. Luckily for that plan, Trotsky was the sort of person who could obsess with little details for weeks and weeks. That's why he had been a perfect Russian socialist.

Bizarre Events

By New Year 1918, the German military were getting seriously annoyed. They knew what Lenin was doing, and Germany was able to split Ukraine off Russia by allying with local nationalists, pushing Russia back. Germany followed this up with demands: they wanted to dominate eastern Europe. They had fought for years to gain vast tracts of eastern land,

and they had beaten Russia, so it was in their minds theirs. Trotsky used this as an excuse to go back to talks with Bolshevik high command. They in turn split three ways: the largest group wanted a revolutionary war against Germany until the whole of Europe was in a class-based civil war (they were known as Left Communists), Trotsky wanted to declare neither war nor peace, leave peace talks and wait and see what happened. Lenin, in the smallest group, wanted to sign a peace treaty. Lenin had to face the fact he was in the smallest camp, and went for the lesser evil in Trotsky's plan. Then the bizarre part began. Trotsky again attended talks and, when Germany was thoroughly annoyed and told him to agree to terms or else … Trotsky told them Russia had left the war and would not sign the peace.

It took a while for Germany to realise how weird this was and react, and they decided to continue the invasion. Lenin lost a vote to sign peace, and on February 18th Germany attacked. They faced no opposition and in one week beat several years' worth of advances. A livid Lenin was afraid of Germany capturing Petrograd, so tried to win a vote to pass the peace. There was heated debate and the Bolsheviks appeared on the verge of their own civil war, but Trotsky conceded, and Lenin won: Russia would sign peace.

But Germany did not stop. They carried on, as if to take the Russian capital, and there was nothing to stop them.

Lenin had to call for soldiers and volunteers, and then he passed a decree which would go on to define communist Russia. He passed 'The Socialist Fatherland in Danger', which allowed the summary execution of the undefined enemy and the ability to use people as forced labour. This began as a response to Germany marching with no restraint into Russia, but turned into a brutal, monolithic system of control and terror. As the Germans closed in on Petrograd, Lenin moved his government to Moscow and took over the Kremlin, a fifteenth-century fortress.

On the 23rd, Germany finally halted (perhaps having heard that the Bolsheviks were seeking out British and French help if they had to restart the war to save their own lives) and offered terms: all the land they had captured, Ukraine and Baltic. Lenin had to win a new debate, but he did, in part when his opposition walked out before a vote (again, again and thrice again). The Treaty of Brest-Litovsk was signed March 3rd. Russia almost ceased to exist as a European power, such was the extent of the losses (until Germany lost the war in the west and the treaty was torn up). Not only did Germany gain huge colonies in the east; they gained massive trade and business rights in Russia, effectively allowing them to run a private business economy alongside the communists' own take on industry. The Bolsheviks were still deeply divided and huge numbers of the old elites and socialist intelligentsia were livid about the surrender. But the Bolsheviks were in power and the war which had wrecked Russia was over, thanks mostly to Lenin's persistence and actual understanding of the situation. With the capital moved to Moscow, there remained a different war to win, a civil war.

The End of Socialism in Russia

Everyone thought the people would grow tired of the Bolsheviks, and they quickly did. As 1918 went on, the workers of the major cities, particularly Petrograd, grew frustrated with continuing food supply problems, the extreme concessions of the peace with Germany, the brutality of the commissars and more. They became so frustrated, in fact, they began forming new factory committees outside the system. Here the Mensheviks and the Right SRs made major gains, and once again a grassroots collection of people turned against the government.

But the Bolsheviks acted differently to the Tsar and the PG, and the Mensheviks acted the same as they always had. With the people wanting to march and take physical action against the Bolsheviks, the other socialists tried to talk them out of action so as not to play into the hands of the Whites in the civil war. As the people tried to march, the Bolsheviks used the army against them, and when it came to soviet elections which the Mensheviks and SRs were about to dominate, the Bolsheviks simply banned them from standing. When they won anyway, the Bolsheviks changed the results to remove them all. In 1918, socialism in Russia died, as the Bolsheviks crushed it and the socialists bowed politely and let it happen. Instead there was only Lenin's new, hybrid dictatorship. Now he abandoned the pretence of all power to the soviets. This was a new state, never seen or theorized before, not even by Marx. It was called by an old name, but given a new meaning: Communism.

CRIB

- The liberals and elites in government won't work with the Bolsheviks, so they create their government at gunpoint.

- The Constituent Assembly is ignored and closed.

- As the working class and peasants explode into a violence born of hate and jealousy, tearing down the upper classes, Lenin takes command and steers it.

- After attempting to string along negotiations, and then having to argue against his own party, Lenin finally brings Russia's part in WWI to a close, with a massive loss of territory.

- The socialist parties are destroyed and soviet, socialist power is ended. The Bolsheviks now rule.

13: The Russian Civil War

Not everyone had stayed to watch the Bolshevik takeover, or even the liberal one months before. People had fled the cities from criminal and revolutionary violence, people had fled the countryside from attacks on their homes and land, people had fled the army after troops became mutinous. In large part, those fleeing were the upper classes: aristocrats, landowners, officers. There were numerous places to run to away from the Bolshevik middle: the east, the south and the west. You could head to a major city that hadn't fallen under Bolshevik control and live like a doomed king. Or, perhaps if you had military experience, you could head to where rebel forces were beginning to gather.

The Battle of Rostov at the end of 1917 was the first major fight of the Russian Civil War. The Don Cossacks had elected General Kaledin as the head of their assembly, the Krug. He had supported Kornilov earlier in 1917, so when Generals Kornilov and Alexeev escaped from Bolshevik eyes they took flight and formed the nucleus of a volunteer 'White' army in the lands of the Don Cossacks. (Some generals had travelled in small groups in disguise, whereas Kornilov had tried to lead a whole unit with him clearly in charge. After one fight too many with the Reds, the unit dispersed and he had to disguise himself and go alone.)

As this small group of volunteers grew via fleeing officers wanting their own revenge, the inherently conservative head of the Krug clashed with the increasingly Bolshevik peasants and workers around him, and then with his own forces who were loath to fight the Red Guards who'd been sent from Moscow to come and take control. Kaledin united his Cossacks with the White troops, who reacted to the Reds' capture of Rostov by retaking it in a six-day battle in December 1917. The Whites had just five hundred men, but they were well trained, and the Reds wilted in the face of opposition. However, the Whites had just as severe problems: they had almost no lower ranking troops so had to become lower ranking troops themselves, leading to massive arguments over rank, which could be found all the way up to the Generals who fell out over the direction of this rebellion against a rebellion.

The Don region didn't need Red Guards marching in to collapse into war, as civil strife tore the region apart, Bolshevik against monarchist. When Red troops did arrive in greater and more trained numbers in February 1918, it became apparent nothing could stop the Whites being pushed away from Rostov. The Whites thus planned a retreat to the still 'rebellious' Kuban region, while Kaledin killed himself. However, the retreat would not be easy.

The Ice March

The flight of the Volunteers from the Don to the Kuban came to be known as the Ice March, a legend in Russian military history. The four thousand-strong volunteer army, accompanied by large numbers of fleeing civilians, trekked from Rostov across frozen steppe in single file with little weaponry and hostile forces all around. They stayed away from the railways, were attacked by villagers and attacked them in turn, both sides committing atrocities, until they closed on Ekaterinodar. Here, they made an alliance with the Cossacks who had been ejected from this city. Seven thousand Whites now tried to siege out over twice that number of Reds. It sounded like a doomed enterprise to many, but Kornilov was adamant his force would capture that city or die trying. Then he died trying, killed by a lucky shell, and General Denikin took charge, decided that he'd rather live than carry on the siege, and led the Whites back the way they'd come. Perhaps oddly, this strengthened the morale and cohesion of (now Denikin's) Whites, as they united in the Ice March, commemorating their dead hero. On the news of Kornilov's death, Lenin announced: "It can be said with certainty that, in the main, the civil war has ended." (Mawdsley, The Russian Civil War, p. 22) He was very wrong.

Also oddly, they returned to a different Don region. Bolsheviks, whether local peasants or interloping Red Guard, had annoyed the old school Cossacks to such an extent they'd rebelled themselves, formed an army and retaken their capital. The Krug had even elected a new leader, General Krasnov and, with German weapons, by summer 1918 Krasnov's Whites were forty thousand in number.

A Nation at War with Itself

The regime change which had begun in Petrograd in 1917 had, by the middle of 1918, spread across the vast Russian Empire. The central cities were the home of this revolution, and areas on the fringes began to break away. Not just through nationalism—which arose to make region after region declare themselves independent states—but also through being pushed into a split from the centre because of anti-Bolshevik forces. Those who had fled – aristocracy, officers, landowners, the middle class – and those who held the same views and already lived on the fringes broke away from the Bolshevik tendrils and almost the whole outlying region of Russia was lost to the revolutionaries. The Treaty of Brest-Litovsk made this worse, because while the Bolsheviks had gained massive support in ending the war from those who were doing the dying in it, the terms – huge regions given to Germany – annoyed monarchists and imperialists. In these fringes, anti-Bolshevik forces coalesced and White armies emerged. However, Lenin had always wanted a bloody civil war in order to crush the many layers of opposition in one mass slaughter, so the fact Bolshevik policy made civil war inevitable was fine, and he didn't try to compromise.

The Czech Legion

There was another force active in Russia. The forty thousand-strong Czechoslovak Legion had been fighting for Russia and the other allies against Germany and Austria-Hungary for independence, and it wanted to carry on the fight even with Russia bowing out. It was thus permitted to leave Russia via the eastern part of the country, where it could travel right round the world and land in western Europe. Things got complicated when the Germans realized the Legion might make it to the Western Front, and put pressure on Bolshevik high command to stop it. They got even more complicated when the forces of the Western Front asked Bolshevik high command to keep the Legion in Russia as part of a renewed Eastern Front. The Legion, oblivious to this, wanted to stick to the plan.

However, the Legion had their weapons and when the Red Army tried to disarm them after a brawl, the Legion resisted then exploded in anger and seized control of local facilities, including the vital Trans-Siberian Railway. Trotsky reacted with the typical calm of a Bolshevik by basically declaring war on them. The Czechs, believing the Bolsheviks wanted to hand them to Germany or just plain kill them, fought back. While the dates of these attacks – May 1918 – are often incorrectly called the start of the Civil War, the Czech legion did swiftly go from allied unit to people in charge of a practical new country, as they had taken a large territory and, with it, railway access to vast areas of Russia. Having been ordered crushed by the Bolsheviks (rather than talked down), the Czechs allied with the Whites in the hope they would win the civil war and restart the fight against Germany again— although these Whites were actually Right SRs who were rebelling in the Volga region. The strange thing about the Whites was, despite the overwhelming evidence that a war against Germany was destroying Russia and making government impossible, the Whites would have tried to fight the Germans again. The Czech Legion had another problem: they were getting messages from the British and French asking them to form a new Eastern Front against Germany, and had to deploy in such a way that they opposed the Reds and the notional German advance. The Czechs' hearts were not in defeating Lenin.

Foreign Involvement

The Bolsheviks faced other foreign involvement, some of it helpful, some of it hindrance. World War One had not ended in the West, and Britain, France and others were still fighting, so hoped to restart the Eastern Front to resume getting at the Central Powers from two major sides. They didn't even want the Russian forces to make a major contribution; they would have been happy with just stopping Germany having free rein in the east. People campaigning for a major Western involvement in the civil war, including Winston Churchill, wanted to help the Whites because the Whites wanted to restart the war and cancel Brest-Litovsk. However, the allies did relatively little at this point, with just the British, French and US landing a small expeditionary force at Murmansk and Archangel. The Germans, in contrast, wanted to keep the Eastern Front closed, keep the gains of their peace treaty and make deals that would turn Russia into an all-you-can-invest buffet for German industrialists. This meant they were interested in supporting anyone who'd do that, and the Bolsheviks seemed most likely.

Given that at one point the Bolsheviks were so desperate for troops they asked if they could use German POWs from World War One as a Red force, you can see where the Germans thought they had an advantage, despite Lenin's statements on the economy and wealth not really matching the dreams of a German empire. Even so, the Germans spoke to White forces as well as Red as they considered all options, and on June 28th, 1918, the Kaiser took the decision of whether to destroy the Bolshevik regime by advancing the small and relatively undefended distance to Petrograd and Moscow, or support it, and give it assurances allowing it to pull troops east to save the civil war. He chose to save it, and the Bolsheviks outlasted his own regime by many decades. It's worth mentioning that at the same time as this, the Reds were flooding Germany with propaganda to try and cause a revolution, and while they had signed secret deals with Germany when they thought the latter would win World War One—deals which gave Germany great involvement in Russia—they rejected those deals shortly after Germany surrendered in the west. Germany wasn't essential in keeping the Bolsheviks in power, but they did play a part with money, weapons and agreeing to look the other way, and if they had won the war would have made great demands of a Russia which would have been their empire. The Germans helped save the Bolsheviks a little, and then the defeat of the Germans helped save them a lot more. For all the talk of Allied intervention and assistance of the Whites, the Allied defeat of Germany was a million times more helpful to the Bolsheviks than the harm of landing troops in the east.

The Germans even gritted their teeth when their ambassador to Russia was assassinated. The last throw of the Left SR's dice occurred when they concluded the Bolsheviks had betrayed the revolution and gathered their forces for a display of opposition. The scheme played out with them challenging the Bolsheviks in congress, walking out when they lost the vote (so far, so normal), and then with the Bolsheviks distracted and Moscow completely open to internal revolt, they assassinated Ambassador Mirbach and … well, that's the thing. Historians have estimated that on those nights, the troops in Moscow loyal to the Left SRs heavily outweighed those of the Bolsheviks, and that they could have arrested Bolshevik high command and tried a seizure of power. Anyone else would have tried a coup. Lenin had. But the Left SRs were ultimately still intellectuals who didn't want to take power; they wanted to trigger the people into expelling the Bolsheviks, and then trigger Germany into a new invasion which would restart the war and be won, somehow magically, by Russia. They lost and ultimately died because they were fantasists and not realists like Lenin and Trotsky. The act of opposition was supressed with one of the great quotes of the revolution: Bolshevik Bukharin to a Left SR: "We were sitting in our room waiting for you to come and arrest us… As you did not do it, we decided to arrest you instead." (Cited from Pipes, *The Russian Revolution,* 1990, p. 642)

The Nature of the Reds

The 'Reds' - the Bolshevik-dominated Red Army, which was hastily formed in 1918 - were clustered around the capital. Operating under the leadership of Lenin and Trotsky,

215

they had a uniform agenda, albeit one that was heavily opposed by major factions below these two leaders, and which changed as the war continued. Lenin and Trotsky were fighting to retain their own control, and keep Russia together under the Bolshevik government. That might sound simplistic, but at least it was more realistic than the Whites and their dreams of the past. The initial Bolshevik impulse had been to reject a formal standing army because they were weapons of control (and yes, control is exactly what the Bolsheviks would use it for), but they soon realized their volunteer worker units of the Red Guard were feckless and wouldn't win any war at all. Trotsky and Bonch-Bruevich (a vital ex-Tsarist commander) pragmatically organized a new Red Army along traditional military lines and used Tsarist officers, despite socialist complaints. The Tsar's former elite joined in droves partly because, with their pensions cancelled, they had little choice and it was better than prison, and latterly because of conscription. Just a few actually wanted to be officers of anything. As you can tell, Lenin and Trotsky only stuck to socialist principles unless they would lose them power, in which case they were suddenly elastic. Others, however, including a man called Stalin who was executing his way through a series of failed specialists, still wanted what they thought was a socialist army with career communists in charge, not ex-aristocratic officers (or, if we're being honest, intellectuals like Trotsky). They formed an official Bolshevik Military Opposition, and because nothing in this book can happen without infighting, they kept up a squabble. Yes, the Red Army was organized by Trotsky on more traditional military lines, but he was surrounded by problematic Bolsheviks who got in the way. Lenin tried to organise a peace deal because he'd rather win the war.

Equally crucial was the Reds' control of the rail network's core, enabling them to move troops around quickly, as well as controlling the key supply regions for both men and material. The Reds' core had sixty million people in a manufacturing and supply heartland, while the Whites very much did not.

Even so, at first the Reds were surrounded and losing the war. Trotsky had given them an officer corps, and now he needed a large army, so he broke another old socialist dream and introduced conscription. He also had the Bolshevik zone declared a giant military camp under military rule and all focus turned to the civil war. Total (civil) war and a new style of economy called War Communism. It was a struggle, but soon millions of (mostly) peasants had been drafted in to fight, and they (mostly) did so because the Whites threatened their land. There were actually more people in the army than the Bolsheviks could equip but numbers had a strength all of their own, an accidental strategy Stalin would ride to success in

217

World War Two. Soldiers who stayed and officers who developed were fiercely indoctrinated into a society that called itself Communism, brutalized into a quasi-military form as the war went on. Lenin had wanted a civil war to allow him to smash the old system and impose a new one. What he got was almost certainly more than he'd planned. But Lenin was still the one ready to fight, destroy and rebuild, while the Whites lived in the past.

The Nature of the Whites

The Whites were a disunited patchwork. They were all opposed to the Bolsheviks but often also to each other, and were totally overstretched thanks to controlling a smaller population over a huge area. They never unified beyond an array of ad hoc groups, operating independently when a group advance might have won them the war and left them with the substantial problem of what to do after. If you're thinking some of them had learned so little from 1917 that they'd call to wait for votes to a Constituent Assembly, you'd be right. The Bolsheviks saw the war as a struggle between their workers and Russia's upper and middle classes, a war of socialism against international capitalism and a battle of their own Red society against the part of society who opposed them. It was a brutal theory, but at least it dealt with what was happening. The Whites, in contrast, were loath to recognise land reforms, so didn't convert the peasants to their cause, and equally loath to recognise nationalist movements, so largely lost fringe support. The Whites were rooted in the old Tsarist and monarchical regime, while Russia's masses had moved on. The Reds had a central command, the Whites were a shattered glass of different factions.

The Whites weren't just a series of unconnected armies; each army was a series of unconnected groups all failing to get on with each other. Generals fought liberals who fought monarchists who fought non-Bolshevik socialists all to gain the upper hand in the direction of the White armies. All had seen their politics fail in 1917, and none realized they would need to solve this again if they were to win the civil war. All the solutions and constitutions and laws they came up with were relics of either the Tsarist era or that of the Provisional Government. To be a White commander fighting a civil war and still, *still* not try and solve the land question was to be doomed, because the Whites never gathered any sense of the people wanted of them, or provided a legitimate alternative to the Reds. Given that the Whites' supporters included all the old large landowners, perhaps they were always doomed. At some point, 'we're not the Reds' fails as a strategy and a new one is needed. It never came, but White Terror was as effective in pushing people to the Reds as Red Terror was in pushing the middle and upper class to the Whites.

Peasant Rebellion

There were also the 'Greens'. These forces fought not for the Reds or the Whites, but after their own goals, like national independence, food and booty, because they didn't want to fight in this war and deserted in opposition to all the brutality ... apart from their own. They were also peasants who had risen in protest of Red Terror and the war the Bolsheviks seemed to be fighting against the rural; Russia. Vast Green armies roamed behind the lines, weakening both sides. In fact, it's likely there were more peasant Greens rebelling against the Bolshevik demands on their village than there ever were White troops. However, the peasants didn't unite very far with each other and certainly didn't march on Moscow (and, really, neither did the Whites, as we shall see). There were also the 'Blacks', the Anarchists.

Civil War

Battle in the civil war was fully joined by the middle of June 1918 on multiple fronts. The Right SRs created The Committee of the Constituent Assembly or 'Komuch, their own republic and government in Volga. Here they had gained support in the Constituent Assembly elections, and were aided greatly by the Czech Legion - but Komuch was a deluded government who postponed every major decision until they could create a new Constituent Assembly to decide it for them. They were still mired in the classic (non-Bolshevik) socialism that thought they needed to install a liberal democracy before they could put in a working soviet. They were mentally doomed before the Reds even arrived.

But this wasn't war in the manner of the Western Front of World War One. There were no fronts, no lines of trenches. There were just stations on the railway lines that armed troops journeyed along until they found opposition they couldn't push off, and then often got pushed back in return.

And now back to the Don. Here, Krasnov had forty thousand troops, with the volunteer army growing and coming up from the south. A group of White commanders were in close proximity and argued about what to do. The result was a perfect microcosm of the White war and why it failed. Krasnov wanted to take their forces and push up to Tsaritsyn on the Volga, and Alexeev wanted to use this to unite with Komuch and the Czech Legion up the Volga. With this force allying with all the others in the region, they could march on Moscow and wipe the Bolsheviks away and install a new government. As a plan it was a good one, but it was never given the chance. Why? Because Denikin decided to be cautious, take his own command, and went back to Kuban to merge his army with Kuban Cossacks to create a larger White army, ready for a later advance on the Bolshevik heartland.

Just when the Whites could have united, they marched in opposite directions. The Cossacks were nationalist and wanted their own new country. The Volunteers wanted an old fashioned Russian empire. The Reds thrived in the gap.

White armies were filled with conscripted troops who spent much of their time walking backwards away from Reds and any actual flying bullets. They had been forced into action by White troops who basically failed to appeal to the peasants they were cajoling on any meaningful level, beyond 'do what we say or we'll shoot some of you', a strategy that fell apart when the Reds were shooting back. Had the White command actually formed a command and put out a policy designed to accept the situation and win the war, these armies might have been much larger and much keener.

Krasnov attacked Tsaritsyn on his own, and while the siege of the city (later known as Stalingrad) caused arguments between the Bolshevik Stalin and Trotsky, an enmity which would greatly affect Russian history, Krasnov alone could not take it. Deniken, with his Volunteer Army and the Kuban Cossacks, had great success with limited numbers against larger, but weaker, soviet forces in the Caucasus and Kuban, destroying a whole soviet army and expanding his force to forty thousand-strong, achieved without allied aid, in charge of a large area. But it was not the Bolshevik heartland, it did not threaten the Bolshevik machine. When Germany withdrew from the Cossacks' southern flank because of the end of World War One, and as Reds advanced, the Don troops were pushed back and on the verge of falling apart. In this sorry, spent state they gave in and allied with Denikin to create the Allied Forces of South Russia, a marvellously inappropriate name. (Only then did Denikin turn to take Kharkov and Tsaritsyn, break out into Ukraine and beginning a general move north towards Moscow. Yes, this provided the greatest threat to the Soviet capital of the war, but yes, his former allies were a shadow of themselves.)

Meanwhile World War One had ended. The Western Allies engaged in foreign intervention suddenly found their key motivation gone, and in a very pleasant manner (they had won the war). France and Italy urged a major military intervention, Britain and the US much less. The Whites urged them to stay, claiming that the Reds were a major threat to Europe, but even after a series of peace initiatives failed, the Europeans definitely weren't sending any troops to do actual fighting. They would send supplies and guards. The importance of the weaponry and equipment imported to the Whites is still debated, as is the consequences of any serious military mission, but there wasn't one.

Back to Komuch, which has been called an experiment; it was more like a freezer for ideas that had already spoiled. The workers thought Komuch too White, the elite too socialist. Land reforms were partially reversed, workers groups were side-lined. Even so, Komuch managed to spread to control millions of people. It just had to persuade them to fight for it. But when Komuch tried to create a People's Army to fight, in the spirit of the French Revolution, the peasants saw no reason to do so as long as they had their land and their village was safe, and the Reds seemed more likely to let them have that land. When conscription was introduced by Komuch, this made things worse, even if it did scrape an army together. Unfortunately, the Reds had used their heartland of sixty million people to form an army twice the size of Komuch. It smashed the People's Army, and Komuch collapsed. It fled east, to Omsk and Siberia. An attempt by Komuch, the Siberian Provisional Government and others in the east to form a unified government produced a five-man Directory in the manner of revolutionary France. That had survived for several years by cunning, but this one had no power, no real base (either in support or to work from), and none of the people involved were happy with it. It lasted eight weeks before a coup took it over, proclaiming Admiral Kolchak Supreme Ruler of Russia (he had no navy and, because nothing in this is straightforward, actually refused the position of dictator before he was talked into it). Kolchak and his right-leaning officers were highly suspicious of any anti-Bolshevik socialists, and the latter were driven out or murdered. The Right SR dream had died. Kolchak then created a military dictatorship. Kolchak was not put in power by foreign allies as the Bolsheviks later claimed; the foreigners were actually against the coup. Japanese troops had also landed in the Far East to secure their own borders, while in late 1918 the French arrived in the Crimea and the British in the Caucuses. They didn't do much.

Methods of Coercion: Terror

The Reds had turned their heartland into a huge war machine, or rather, they'd tried to. If you're wondering how the Russian army of World War One had failed to supply a multimillion-strong army and feed its cities, and how the Reds were doing this, the answer was they hadn't either. Food was growing scarce in the urban centres: the cities had been fed mostly by large farms, but these had been broken up and shared out by peasants who couldn't, or wouldn't, match the production. The many reasons food had grown scarce in World War One were repeated, and people went on strike and protested. Now, however, with their Bolshevik government and little hope of a different one, millions of people either fled to the country to live with the food, or formed groups who would scavenge what they could and make purchases in private from the country. A market of desperate trade grew up, and this was anathema to the Bolsheviks.

Their answer wasn't socialism, it was a system they invented and later called War Communism which combined economics with terror: no private trade, all industry taken over by the state, and food production collectivized, money replaced with rationing, a state-run and state-controlled system very much at the point of a gun and designed, not for worker fairness or any other socialist ideal, but to wage war as best it could. Food was taken by force from the farmers in a combination of desperation but also the inevitable bitter end and hatred begun when the going to the peasants movement of the last century had failed.

There was death of independent trade unions, factory committees and the legal right to strike, aka the workers' weapons. A war, not just against the Whites, but against those within their heartland, to take control. Let's look at the peasants: the Whites refused to settle the land issue and suggested they might send the land back to the rich, so the peasants stayed away. The Reds used their actions and attacks to promise to keep seizure land seized, waging a war of submission on the peasants in order to destroy those who preferred SRs and non-Bolshevik groups, make the peasants obey, and to gather food. They created a theoretical split between evil, capitalist, hoarding and profiting peasants— called 'kulaks'—and good, honest, poorer peasants, and set the cities to war against the kulaks using the old fashioned human qualities of hate and jealousy. It didn't matter there weren't really kulaks, because when Lenin promised death to them suddenly fewer urban workers wanted rid of him as they were focused on the mythical rural baddies you could pin so many wrongs on. No one listened to your screams if you'd been branded a kulak, certainly not in the city heartlands of Bolshevik support. That the Bolsheviks failed to make the poor peasants destroy the rich led to full Red grain armies, plundering the countryside to do it instead. But this iron- and blood-stained fist kept the Bolsheviks in control just enough. That the Bolsheviks didn't actually want peasants holding land anyway, that they planned to introduce state-run collective farms where peasants were workers whenever they could in the future, was not a secret but still did not outweigh the Whites. (Also, it's interesting to note the urban war on the rural peasant wasn't a Bolshevik invention; Robespierre for one had already thought of it in the French Revolution.)

In the cities, Mensheviks and SRs fed militant workers in protests against the Bolsheviks. The nationalization of industry wasn't just Bolshevik theory, it was the party and the state taking control from workers' groups who were rebelling, crushing that rebellion with guns and layers of government. The Whites failed to make enough promises or use enough force in their regions. The Bolsheviks kept enough big cities filled with millions of workers onside, and enough of the

227

millions of peasants afraid of White land seizures to fight despite brutalising others. The Whites never achieved either.

The Whites lacked something else the Reds had: the Cheka, a secret police dedicated to torture, murder and enforcing a deliberate policy of Red Terror to maintain control. This was the broken glass of class war, the killing state machine that shadowed every other state department and aspect of human life, a vast society of its own. While it operated outside the law by Western standards, it operated under a new system in Russia which scrapped the entire pre-1917 legal system and created a new one of fake trials that could execute anyone on a judge's whim. More commonly, you could just get shot by a Cheka officer you had upset. In theory, the Red Terror was launched after Lenin was shot in a failed assassination attempt, but in practice that was when it simply got worse. It was a key aspect of Communist rule, a war against society to make it subservient. Hundreds of thousands were killed by the Cheka. Concentration camps were created, and thousands incarcerated in them and threatened into forced labour; they were not a Stalinist invention (or, for that matter, a Nazi one), although Stalin would go on to vastly expand the Gulags. Lenin had always had a coldness and hate which allowed him to argue for campaigns of state extermination, and now he led them. The terror was partly inspired by Robespierre's version in the

French Revolution, and partly by the Bolsheviks pushing it to new extremes because they wanted a war on their very population and society to make it obedient and cleanse the hate in their souls.

You can get into a historical debate here about whether War Communism was Lenin being pragmatic while his real views on economy were the mixed ones of 1918 and after the civil war, or whether this was what he really wanted and those other periods were when he backed off. The Bolsheviks were anti-market in writing, but Lenin kept trying to keep one, so how much of this was also an attempt to seize and control the peasants and workers in a way the Whites never managed? War Communism failed in an economic sense by almost every measure. The industrial output of Russia fell by over 70%, the urban population was greatly reduced and starvation killed millions. It failed in the psychological sense too, its terror not binding the workers or the peasants to the state. Richard Pipes is adamant that the Bolsheviks wanted this system and only backed off to save themselves, but his work on the subject has always described a chaos that does seem to mean War Communism was an ad hoc reaction in a party and country at war with itself. These intellectuals had very little in the way of experience when it came to running an economy or country, and had focused on revolution over government. So many of the actions the Bolsheviks took in 1917 to 1921 seemed to be desperate gestures in the direction of what they wanted, affected by what might keep them in power. They started with poorly thought-out ideas which were brutalized by war, desperation and the threat of their imminent destruction.

The interpretation you choose colours how you view the next two decades of Russian history, and I would go for a middle ground that incorporates both. Lenin was pre-disposed to try something like this, but the Bolsheviks allowed themselves to be shaped by the conditions of the war more than people realise, clung to it for longer than they needed because the war had bent them into this shape. In the New Economic Policy, they once more changed to meet demand. The traits in Lenin that allowed him to take power made what followed incredibly likely.

The Height of the Whites

The Reds attacked Ukraine, where Ukrainian nationalists were fighting them for independence (but often still socialist government). The situation soon broke down into a territorial division of rebel forces in some areas and the Reds in others, all under a puppet Ukrainian leader.

We welcome back into the narrative (former Prince) Lvov, who had survived the early Red Terror by the skin of this teeth, started working for Kolchak, and met with US President Woodrow Wilson to ask for America's help in the civil war. When this was refused he went to the post-war talks crafting the Treaty of Versailles, although 'crafting' suggests an art and not the use of oversized hammers. His persuasion was partly responsible for the World War One allies sending vast amounts of aid, including ammunition to Kolchak. No troops who would do any substantive fighting, but certainly enough equipment for Kolchak to stage a major offensive designed to show the West their money wasn't being wasted and they could win this thing. How could the Whites lose? They were liberating a population experiencing terror. An attack began.

Kolchak and multiple armies attacked from the Urals towards the west, made some gains, stalled as supply lines extended, as locals rejected them and as the weather turned, then were pushed back. The White army was having trouble getting troops and supplies to the front, so they took what they could and alienated the peasants as fast or faster than the Reds did. The Red Terror's morale sapping found a rival in what looked suspiciously like Tsarist forces stepping out of the history books and calling themselves Whites when it came to repelling peasant support. The further the Whites advanced, the more peasants they found who wanted to keep the land or die in the process, which the Reds, as remarkable as it seemed, offered the better chance of. So, the Whites resorted to White Terror to make peasants feed them and fight: executing whole

231

villages, kidnapping young men and more, which triggered peasant rebellions and Green armies in the White rear too. Kolchak's forces were pushed back so far they abandoned Omsk, intending to resume business in Irkutsk, but Kolchak was stranded, declared an enemy by a self-proclaimed Siberian government, resigned, got captured by the Czechs and was handed over along with gold in exchange for the Czech Legion's exit from the continent, before being executed.

When Kolchak had been at his best, Denikin had been attacking as well. But not to Tsaritsyn and the Volga where he could have linked with Kolchak, not yet; he kept defending the Don region and the Cossack people from a Red army which had marched in search of ethnic cleansing. That really pushed the Cossacks into the White forces, and Denikin's whites finally managed to advance into Ukraine and the Volga. Of course, it was too late to link up with the rest of the White armies, one of the things the Reds dreaded, but it was still a breakthrough. Denikin was notionally in charge of three advancing armies, and he now issued the Moscow Directive: a triple-pronged advance up to the Red capital, to cut them off and destroy them. This wasn't even popular among all of Denikin's commanders, let alone anyone else, and where one commander would fear the White advance being too dispersed, too drawn away from supplies and too far away from consolidated bases, another commander would ensure all those things happened as they grabbed land. Even so, Denikin's Whites got to within 250 miles of Moscow, their greatest point of success.

In fact, there was even a co-ordinated attack as the Northwestern Army, which was small but skilled under Yudenich, advanced out of the Baltic and threatened St. Petersburg at the same time. However, Yudenich had alienated the Finns and their army by not agreeing to their independence, and faced none other than Trotsky in person motivating the people of the old capital. Trotsky won, and once-upset workers surged out to defend the revolution. A counter attack blunted the Whites and pushed them back so hard they quit.

Defeat and Victory

Back with Denikin, the Whites simply ran out of troops to sustain the advance, to guard and pacify the regions conquered, to make their entire system work. They could not persuade or threaten enough people to fight for them. Denikin had marched through Ukraine, could have saved Ukraine from the Bolsheviks and used local nationalism to come to an agreement with the locals. It needn't be independence, but it could have been. Instead Denikin approached Ukrainians like servants in a Russian fief. He wouldn't even use the name of

233

the place. Not only did the Ukrainians not come out in force to fight for the Whites, they fought against them (albeit for themselves and not the Reds, but it still weakened the Whites and benefitted the Reds). With overstretched supply lines, the Whites tried to gather supplies from the regions they advanced into, and ended up inflicting a brutal White Terror of murders and thefts on locals who didn't feel that liberated at all. In fact, as the Whites closed on Moscow and the arms production capital of Tula, deserters returned to the Red Army to defend 'the revolution' and land reform from the Whites. The Bolsheviks, realising what was happening, offered amnesties to people who came back. The Reds grew stronger, the Whites ran out of everything and a Red counter forced them to retreat. The tide had turned for the final time.

Beaten back to the coast, the White commanders blamed Denikin. As the army tried to evacuate to Crimea, Denikin was forced by his junior commanders not just to resign, but to appoint in his place a man he'd just sent away in disgrace: Wrangel. Denikin fled abroad. The struggle would go on, but by early 1920 the war was practically over. The Whites no longer had a chance. But many people would die before they gave up, and for the Reds something extraordinary happened. Former General Brusilov, the hero of World War One, had resisted the chance to join the Whites because he felt the Russian people had, for better or worse, chosen the Reds.

234

His son had been executed by the Whites fighting for the Reds, and Brusilov followed the young man: he joined the Red Army command. He was alarmed at the imperial invasion the newly formed Poland had begun, and wished to defend Russia from them. Now, with Brusilov as a figurehead, revolutionary socialists in Russia finally called on Russian patriotism to inspire the troops and, unlike all liberal attempts to do this in 1917, people reacted. Over ten thousand officers saw Brusilov with them and the Poles invading and signed up for the Reds.

Lenin ordered an attack into Poland when the Reds stopped the Polish invasion. This wasn't, as Richard Pipes has argued, the start of an attempt to conquer Europe and Bolshevise the lot, but an attempt to blunt what he thought was a Western puppet-state in Poland and show the West they should not interfere anymore with the Reds. If the West erupted in revolution, well, the Red Army would march on in time for tea and medals, not actually start it at all. That the attack on Poland failed and a hasty peace was drawn up meant the lesson wasn't given, but it was a while longer before a European decided on a major adventure into the Russian heartland (a German called Hitler). That the attack on Poland failed because the Reds could not stir the locals to fight for revolution was just a reflection of the Russian Civil War, albeit in reverse. In other, newly national, states on the outskirts of Russia, Red forces marched in and imposed government from Moscow, but only partly from a desire to hold the Russian Empire together, and partly because they had to in order to defeat the Whites and others, like Georgia's Menshevik government. Here the Reds ruled by promoting locals who had joined the party, pushing a nationalized Bolshevism which was both amenable to the area and listening to the centre.

By summer 1920, Wrangel and the last of the Whites were in Crimea, ruling through White Terror. Wrangel tried some land reform, but it was too little too late, and a final advance was blunted. Tens of thousands of people fled abroad as the Reds advanced and crushed the last White region.

By the end of the Civil War, Russia had millions of bureaucrats running the state, controlling every aspect of life, a huge support base of party people. Lenin and the Politburo ran it from the top, centralization was the order of the day, Kafkaesque control was the reality. Literate peasant ex-soldiers flooded into the ranks of the party, a new ruling elite which felt to the non-elite like they were actually part of the same people, unlike in the Tsar's regime. They had to struggle to control a peasantry and workforce deeply angry over their treatment during the civil war. This was complicated by the dreams of leading communists to reformat Russian civilization along utopian (albeit, to many dystopian) ideals which seemed like science fiction, and which satirists did turn into science fiction.

With the Whites gone, the countryside, the workers and even the Kronstadt sailors erupted in a vast revolt against the Bolsheviks, now rebranded as the Communist Party. Lenin admitted that this was more dangerous than any White force, and finally stepped back from War Communism to introduce the semi-market New Economic Policy. That, however, is for a different book, although there's a brief appendix on it later.

CRIB

- With the Bolsheviks in control of a core central region, rebel 'White' armies form in the periphery.

- The Reds might be a unified force under strong central control, but the Whites are disparate and divided, wanting different things from each other let alone the Reds.

- A civil war is waged between the 'two', complicated by the Greens, who are vast numbers of rebels against both sides and operate behind the front lines.

- The Reds are pragmatic, organized by Trotsky into a modern army using Tsarist officers and conscription. They employ Red Terror to keep their grasp on the population.

- The Reds' policies, dubbed War Communism, involve complete state control of industry and army units taking grain at gunpoint.

- The Whites fail to solve the land question, and even their White Terror fails to control a population they might have liberated, if the locals didn't prefer the Reds and their approval of land seizures.

- With interior lines, a denser population and an industrial heartland, the Reds fight off the Whites because the latter never co-ordinate their attacks. Individual White forces come close to a breakthrough, but get beaten in turn.

14: Conclusions

The Russian Revolution was not inevitable, and the final victory of the Bolsheviks even less so. Yes, Russia was being stressed by wide-ranging pressures, from industrialization, urbanization and Westernization, to needing reform to fight modern wars properly, but only at the very end had things reached a stage where they could not have been averted. None of those pressures, from massive amounts of new workers to ever-more eyes on political ideas like liberalism and socialism, meant Russia would definitely revolt. A more pragmatic Tsar could have steered the way to liberal reform at any number of points before 1917, and I'm not talking about 'axe the monarchy' sort of reforms. Britain had and still has a monarchy, despite being a nation run by Parliament, and Russia wouldn't even have had to go that far. But in Nicholas II Russia found itself with a man determined to rule as an autocrat, with absolutely no concessions, looking firmly at the past.

Yet the presence of Nicholas didn't make the revolution inevitable. In 1905, St. Petersburg was the scene of what could have been a revolution, but the military stayed loyal, Nicholas made a few half-hearted attempts at concessions and Russia continued under the Tsar. The Duma might have evolved into something which would negate further revolution given time.

However, by 1917, many chances had been missed and now an uprising was inevitable, though not necessarily a Bolshevik one. The change, and the trigger, was war. The conflict had gone so badly for Russia, the government had been seen to fail so badly, the Tsar and the disaster were so closely linked that there was going to be stiff opposition and, given Russian history, mass strikes. But unlike 1905, by 1917 the war had hardened and repelled so many soldiers that they rebelled along with the workers, and the Tsar was in the end forced away by his Generals and the leading politicians who acted from fear of being swept aside by a tide of popular resentment not yet guided by professional socialists. So Russia had rebelled, and two sources of government were formed: the Provisional Government and the Soviet.

They did not have to fail. The Bolsheviks, who began as a fringe party, did not have to win. The problem was the people now in charge of Russia, in this hybrid dual government, just weren't very good at ruling. The nation had been bound under the Tsar for so long that few had any conception of how to run a functioning empire, let alone a newly liberal or socialist one, and almost all of them maintained entirely wrong opinions about the war. The liberals in Russia found themselves in charge of a country they were

240

partly afraid of (in terms of the socialist masses), with dreams of victory in war still lodged in their heads. If the PG had called for an armistice in March, there may never have been another revolution. The Soviet was in a similar place: it was filled by people who'd spent their lives planning for revolution, in opposition, but they were just not psychologically ready to assume power. They were mentally blocked, and they too avoided the war. Everyone began to be seduced by military victory, and hoped a Constituent Assembly would magically bring everyone together. Furthermore, it's popular now to regard socialists as cold, murderous people thanks to Stalin and Lenin's takes on communism, but throughout this narrative you'll have seen how most socialists consistently refused to destroy Bolshevism, a nakedly violent and hostile force, out of a misplaced sense of brotherhood. Most socialists argued over points of party structure and liked walking out. They were too nice to crush the Bolsheviks even when the latter were planning an armed takeover. How could the mass of Russian socialists ever have ruled the Russia they inherited in 1917?

Why did the Bolsheviks take power in October? The Tsar failed again and again to react to the fault lines in his empire and was swept away by people who failed again and again to react to the fault lines in their new democracy. Only Lenin maintained what seemed to be an answer: no war and land transfer. Even so, the Bolsheviks seized control of a grassroots opposition rather than taking power in their own name, and they had to fight a bloody civil war and install a murderous police state to solidify that power in their own name. But unlike everyone else in 1917—even the egomaniacal but ultimately non-psychotic Kerensky—Lenin had the right combination of pragmatism and a willingness to commit murder to put this regime in place. He'd spent many years shouting loudly about revolution and armed seizures of power and suffered his own mental block (if not fear) in the middle of 1917, but when he committed to taking power he went all-out, bending through War Communism and Tsarist military to New Economic Policy to stay in charge. He was one of the few willing to fight a civil war, to kill to keep power, to adapt. Liberals, other socialists, even some Bolsheviks and monarchists could not keep pace. For Marx, the economy determined the type of government; Lenin would use the government to impose the type of economy, not once but twice. Lenin was not brutalized by the years of civil war: he had started that way. He could have been stopped in mid-1917 easily enough, he might have been beatable in the civil war, but the opposition was divided, ineffectual and in the wrong mindset.

In a sense, the Bolsheviks solved the problems the Romanovs had faced in the first part of the twentieth century by applying more pressure, and exerting more bloody control than the Tsar had. Nicholas II, reluctant to shed any of his authoritarian power, couldn't commit to murder the way the Communists did. He failed, and they succeeded in the medium term.

The Fate of the Romanovs

Nicholas II had refused to leave Russia without his family, if that had even been a real option, and an opportunity arose to go to Britain. However, while the British royal family had initially accepted the idea of offering the Tsar sanctuary, they soon changed their minds under political pressure from within their country. Nicholas ended up being known in the post-February era simply as Nicholas Romanov, and he and his large family were arrested and confined in a large building at Tsarskoe Selo. Here they had limited freedom: they could dine well, but they could not freely walk the grounds. The family amused themselves with games, reading and the occasional visit from politicians like Kerensky. If accounts are to be believed, the newly powerless Nicholas found a freedom and enjoyment in this imprisonment / confinement he had never experienced before. Truly, he had never been suited to the role of Tsar and was always better as a country squire.

This period of gentrified containment didn't last long. The Petrograd Soviet wanted the former royals symbolically locked in the Peter and Paul Fortress, others wanted them away from the heart of revolution, some wanted them executed, and very few wanted them in exile where an opposition could grow around them. They were instead sent to a former governor's property in Tobolsk. This had the advantage of being away from the power struggles in St. Petersburg and Moscow (and not on a railway line so random passing troops wouldn't arrive), but the great misfortune of being near Ekaterinburg, which in 1918 became controlled by very militant Bolsheviks, some of whom wanted to march down and start executing.

The royal family became caught in a complicated web. Trotsky was hoping to bring Nicholas to the capital, put him on trial and have a very grand affair. This led to a bizarre episode where an agent of the central Bolsheviks was sent out to collect the royal family without the extremely militant local Bolsheviks being aware. This plan went wrong and after tense discussion, ended with the royal family remaining in Ekaterinburg and being controlled by the locals. Here they were frequently mocked, and waited to find out their fate. On the one hand, the locals promised to keep them alive and await orders. On the other, there was a civil war raging. Equally, when Nicholas was told he was being taken away, he thought it was because Lenin and the others needed him to sign the Treaty of Brest-Litovsk. He was still in a fantasy world. The ex-Tsarina decided to leave behind her beloved and sick son to support her husband. While imprisoned in Ekaterinburg, contact with the outside world was cut off, to the extent of painting over the windows and erecting a huge fence round the perimeter of the manor. The guards were former urban workers but had machine guns.

Wanting to deny the Whites control of the royal family and permanently end the question of what to do with them, Bolshevik central command came round to the same way of thinking as the militant locals: the royal family needed to be erased. This was partly because White forces would reach Ekaterinburg in just days and temporarily take control, and because the central Bolsheviks had decided a show trial was not just unnecessary, but actively harmful to their cause and command. The royal family would not become a grand example to Russia, they would just vanish. A test execution was staged, with a Grand Duke imprisoned elsewhere taken into the woods, shot, and reported as trying to escape. Nobody in the cities seemed that worried by the news. Lenin ordered the executions of Nicholas and his immediate family.

This was why, on July 4th, the secret police (the Cheka) took over the Romanovs' protection. The night of July 16th saw Cheka officers wake the ex-Tsar and his companions, consisting of his wife, son, four daughters, their doctor and three servants, as well as the family dog. All eleven people were led to the basement (the pretence that they were being anything other than executed saw the former royals given time to wash and dress), where they were shot and stabbed repeatedly. Once all had died (and all did die, despite later legends), the corpses were stripped, abused and dumped in shallow graves, then doused in acid and moved to different graves. Many other members of the Romanov family were killed around this time in other parts of Russia.

The Bolsheviks admitted the Tsar was dead but lied about everyone else, to widespread disinterest. The soviets only admitted the royal women were dead several years later, and the bodies remained undiscovered until decades after. The house was demolished in 1977 as it was on the verge of becoming a monarchist shrine, and the local soviet even held a show trial of the killers, which didn't include any of the real killers. Several people would claim to be an escaped Princess Anastasia, but none were. She died along with the rest.

Nothing is more emblematic of the way Bolshevik policy went during the years of the civil war than them wanting a grand show-trial then turning around and making the Romanovs the victims of the Red Terror, dumping their bodies, along with millions of other people, without fanfare.

Grigori Rasputin

It's unclear how much of a role Rasputin played in the downfall of the Romanov dynasty. Some historians are sceptical he made any difference, while on the other extreme we have Kerensky, who survived the revolution in exile and gave his own side of the story. For him, without Rasputin creating rumours of moral corruption among the royals and causing chaos with the politicians, there would have been no Lenin (but presumably he'd hope for still some Kerensky).

Early Life

The details of Rasputin's early years are sketchy, partly because he made up an awful lot of stories about it and kept everything deliberately confused. He was definitely born into a family of Siberian peasants, probably in the 1860s. He liked to say he first developed 'mystical skills' when he was twelve, but we know he did badly at school and drifted into a life of criminality. Supporters say his reputation from this era is false, and that he took the name Rasputin from the Russian for 'crossroads', while everyone else is in general agreement that 'Rasputin' comes from the Russian for 'dissolute', because he was a drunkard, womaniser, thief, thug and rapist.

Travels

Rasputin married and had several children, before something happened to him. On the one hand, you could believe the common story that he had a religious epiphany and took himself off to a monastery, or you could believe the more basic claim that he was forced into one as a punishment. Either way, he didn't become a real monk, and he ended up in literally the worst place he could possibly have gone. Siberia has a tradition of what is most politely described as extreme mysticism, and Rasputin found himself in a cult of masochistic religious extremists who believed you had to shed your earthly passions to become close to God. The way to achieve this was to become sexually exhausted. Needless to say, Rasputin joined in. He might then have had a vision, albeit more psychological than religious, and travelled throughout Eastern Europe performing healings and prophecies while living off donations and liaisons. He did return to Siberia, but then moved off again.

Rasputin and the Tsar

Rasputin came to St. Petersburg around 1903, finding it fertile ground. The Russian court (and aristocracy) was in the middle of an esoteric fashion trend, and anything suitably occult appealed, especially holy men of peasant stock. The royal court often invited mystics and other quasi-religious figures in, falling under their spell, with one con artist even convincing Nicholas II he was able to contact his dead father. Rasputin presented himself as an unkempt mystic, with piercing eyes and an unusual but genuine charisma. He met with aristocrats and was introduced to the court in the hope that the Romanovs would find him interesting and reward the aristocrats who took him. Rasputin was the perfect person at the perfect time, meeting the Tsar and Tsarina in 1905. He was accepted and began to carve out a niche at court.

The key event of Rasputin's life occurred in 1908. The Tsar's son was a haemophiliac, and during one episode of bleeding, Rasputin was called to assist. When he succeeded (not from magic but perhaps because his charisma was able to calm the boy), he played his cards well and told the Romanovs that the boy, the dynasty and their futures were linked to him, the mystic. Desperate for their son to be cured and thinking they'd just seen a glimpse of it, they felt a debt had been created and built a strong connection. This only increased in 1912 through sheer chance: the boy fell ill after an accident and then a jarring coach ride, and although Rasputin wasn't near, he claimed to have helped the boy through prayer and God. The boy recovered quite coincidentally from the near-fatal illness, but the Tsarina was devoted.

It was slightly more complex than just helping those two. The royal family were trying to turn away from modernity and embrace a quasi-medieval style of rule which valued peasant life, autocracy and the past. As the pair felt increasingly alone in the world, they welcomed Rasputin as the ideal of this. He lived with his daughters, brought over from Siberia.

Rasputin: Royal Favourite

Rasputin almost certainly never slept with the Tsarina, but the people of St. Petersburg weren't so lucky. During his time as royal favourite, he lived a double life, pretending to be a humble peasant around the Tsarina, but finding great pleasure in seducing, even humiliating, noble women, sleeping with prostitutes and drinking massively. The Romanovs were firm believers in the image of the noble common man and the Tsar didn't just refuse to listen to accusations of debauchery: he even exiled accusers. Compromising photographs were spirited away. In 1911 things had become so bad that Prime Minister Stolypin, never a man to back away from a confrontation with the Tsar, produced a report on the mystic's actions. The Tsar had it vanished, because the Tsarina was still desperate for her son and completely beholden to Rasputin, and the Tsar was pleased to see his wife and son calmed.

Royal patronage was still powerful, and hundreds of people came to visit him for magical treatment, and more earthly desires: they were called Rasputinki. Even his fingernail clippings, black with filth, were considered relics. He was a living legend across the empire, and as an early adopter of the telephone, he could be reached for advice that way.

Rasputin in Command

It wasn't all going well. As the events which turned into World War One developed, Rasputin was stabbed and taken to hospital. To his credit, he was against going to war, but this only lasted until he realized the Tsar was going to mobilise his troops, so he did a quick U-turn and supported it. Intriguingly, Rasputin appears to have started to doubt his own power and felt he was fading, needing to work to keep the Tsarina's faith (and his own position). Then, in 1915, the Tsar decided the best way to deal with the war was to put himself in direct charge and travel to the front. He left behind the civilian government and put the Tsarina in charge of internal affairs. The Tsarina effectively put Rasputin in charge instead.

Officially the Tsarina's advisor but in practice kingmaker, he used his power to appoint and fire politicians and ministers of the government, and he did so on his whim. Consequently there was a revolving door, with people coming and going unrelated to any ability, unable to learn the job before they were gone. The result was chaos, utter chaos, and the props were further kicked out from underneath the Romanov regime. This was not a benevolent Tsar or Tsarina, this was abuse.

Murder

There had been attempts on Rasputin's life before 1916, but all had failed. However, the chaos in government provoked supporters of the Tsar and his autocratic regime to try and murder Rasputin before he could do any more damage, because they could see a link between the mystic's actions and growing calls to replace the Tsar. A Prince, a Grand Duke and a Duma member were among those who dreamt up the plot, which might have had a personal grievance embedded into it: the ringleader may have approached Rasputin for help with being gay. Either way, Prince Yusupov invited Rasputin over, where he was served poisoned food, then shot and shot again as he tried to escape. Once dead, he was tied up and thrown into the Neva River. When the body was found he was buried twice but dug up each time, and eventually cremated at the side of a road.

Lenin

Childhood

Vladimir Ilich Ulyanov was born in Simbirsk, Russia, on April 22nd, 1870. The name 'Lenin' was adopted in 1901, probably after the River Lena. There might only have been a very narrow middle class in Russia, but Lenin was born into it. Not only was his father educated and liberal, but as a teacher who had been promoted to inspector of schools, he was both a government bureaucrat and a member (albeit at the bottom end) of the hereditary nobility. In terms of heritage, his father had Mongol ancestry. The happy, comfortable life was reflected in a Lenin who displayed a gift for learning and languages. Four of his siblings reached adulthood, and, perhaps oddly, all became revolutionaries.

Lenin's Life Changes

Lenin did well at school, was devout and in the early phase of his life had no political leanings, even though he would later claim to have been a socialist. Then two events changed his life, and historians generally recognise these as key in setting Lenin on a revolutionary course. Firstly, his father was pressured to retire early by the Tsarist government because they were scared of public education. Although his father died in 1866 before he'd been forced out, the stresses were there. Perhaps more importantly, Lenin's older brother had joined a revolutionary group planning to assassinate Tsar Alexander III, been arrested and then executed. It's easy to see how these could have caused Lenin to explore political issues, and he read books like *What Is To Be Done?*, which set out a model for revolutionaries: fanatical, devoted, harsh. Initially, Lenin was a Populist. In 1887 Lenin went to university in Kazan after his previous school provided references to stress he wasn't like his elder brother.

Of course, now he *was* like his elder brother, and three months into university Lenin was expelled for illegal activities. He was then arrested and sent to his family home for punishment. He was allowed back to Kazan in 1888, but refused a return to university, even though many positions of employment were now closed due to his reputation. Instead of work, Lenin began to read (this would become a common theme), and in 1889 he not only rejected Populism, he became a Marxist. Even at this stage he wasn't a devoted Marxist, as he read widely and took on board Marx's rivals. The ideas Lenin produced in the famous part of his career are influenced as much by Russia's own revolutionary tradition as by Marx and his western writing. Lenin was the sort of person who had no problem adapting Marx to fit his own point of view.

The family moved to Samara in 1889, and Lenin went back to university. He obtained a first-class law degree and permission to practice law.

Exile in Siberia

Despite considering the Russian legal system to be filled with 'class bias', Lenin worked as a lawyer. He moved to St. Petersburg in 1893 where he connected with Marxists and other socialists. He turned himself into a revolutionary, and in 1895 went to Western Europe to discuss rebellion with Russian exiles. It was subsidized by his mother's pension, paid by the Russian government he was far from keen on. When back in the capital he worked to unify Marxist groups to better agitate for change. However, in 1895 the leaders of this new union were arrested, including Lenin, and he was jailed for fifteen months and exiled to Siberia for three years. Lenin married a comrade from the Marxist struggle, Nadezhda Krupskaya, so she could come with him. They remained married, although there appears to have been no real intimacy, just a lifelong support for the revolution.

Exile in Siberia was relatively nice, with a housekeeper, a village to roam around in and guns to hunt with. However, prison has a habit of changing people, and as Lenin read and developed his political views, he went back to the heroes of revolutionary literature and suppressed his hobbies to focus entirely on the revolution. He succeeded. While Trotsky would claim that the Lenin of 1917 was made in this period, Lenin still exhibited more human emotions than he later would. The harshness had yet to fully develop.

The Bolsheviks

When he was released from Siberia, Lenin took a common action for Russian revolutionaries: he moved to Western Europe. Here, he had an easier time of being a revolutionary, and he joined other exiled Marxists to start a newspaper to promote their thinking (which was still developing). It was called *Iskra*, or *The Spark*. They realized that a newspaper was a great way to build a party and explain core thoughts, and the editors of *Iskra* were central figures of the Russian Marxist scene.

Lenin did not toe any party line, and came up with theoretical solutions to problems which, as we've seen, stifled other socialists right until their end. For instance, how a rural nation with a small urban proletariat could have a Marxist revolution. In his 1902 book *What Is To Be Done?* Lenin also outlined how a centralized party would be needed to make a revolution and lead workers. While the volume isn't the fully-fledged Bolshevik manifesto which defined 1917 (which is what it can look like), it's interesting to note Lenin would take the same line in power as he did in opposition: a small hard core of dedicated people, led by him.

With *Iskra* growing in popularity, the leaders of the Russian Marxist groups tried to unify themselves as the Russian Social-Democratic Workers' Party (RSDWP), but they failed utterly. The first attempt at a general congress was in Minsk in 1898 and didn't work, but a second congress in London became a defining moment in Russian and world history. The party divided, partly because Lenin demanded a party led by devoted revolutionaries, whereas the rest wanted a much more inclusive structure. His opposition worried his plan would create a dictatorship, and despite all the other things they got wrong, here they were very right. Lenin's supporters were united around him, while the rest had no clear leader, but Lenin was in the minority. However, the opposition walked out of the congress, giving him a majority of who was left in the room, and so his faction became known as the Majority: Bolsheviks. Lenin had demonstrated no love or support of a young political party, making enemies to ruthlessly promote himself and his ideas. The split would never be healed.

1905 and Beyond

The Mensheviks (as the actual majority of the party was known) were unable to heal the rift because Lenin was

259

impossible to please. He alienated every other major grouping in European socialism, resigned from *Iskra* in a protest, and set about building a new generation of socialists that looked to him as leader. He wasn't in Russia when the attempted revolution of 1905 began, and only arrived ten months after it had begun. Clearly too late to do any good, he went back into exile in 1907 having contributed only theory, and certainly no physical revolution. Fans of little historical details might wish to note how he nearly died on the exit journey when he was literally on thin ice.

Lenin formalized the party split when he called his own Bolshevik congress in 1912, but he was an energetic and constant campaigner, providing a wealth of articles, alienating more people and keeping his party small.

World War One and 1917

The outbreak of World War One produced a surprising reaction among many European socialists, with many pledging to support their national governments in the war effort. Ever the contrarian, Lenin was against the war from the beginning, calling it an imperialist and capitalist war which workers should revolt against rather than die en masse in. Lenin began to hope World War One would turn into a European civil war in which the workers ejected the upper class who wanted them to fight. This didn't happen, and Lenin managed to end up in a smaller and more alienated minority than ever before.

As the war continued, Lenin lived in neutral Switzerland. A few weeks before February 1917, he said that he might never live to see the Russian Revolution, and was spectacularly embarrassed when it happened soon after. What happened next has been covered by the rest of this book. However, when Lenin arrived in Russia after being ferried along by Germans, people who had known him before the exile noted how he had changed: a harsh, cold man set solely on ruling. He agitated for a seizure of power but didn't have the nerve to do it during the July Days, finally realising his last chance was coming in October.

The Bolshevik seizure of power had a lot to do with the failures of the socialists and liberals to tackle key problems, but it would never have happened without Lenin being Lenin: a man who purposefully drove the doubting members of his party into a coup.

There were many revolutionaries and intellectuals in the Bolsheviks, but, with the exception of Trotsky (who would win the civil war with his brutal yet effective / brutally effective vision of battle), none would have pushed the party into the actions of 1917 without Lenin. He alone was prepared to wage a civil war against his own people to secure his power. He alone was happy with that idea. Lenin's genius was

261

partly having the bloody realism to do what was needed to secure his goals, something lacking among the other players of 1917.

Final Years

Lenin had to fight the civil war he'd wanted, and during this a brutalized, authoritarian state emerged. Historians argue whether the real Lenin was the man behind the New Economic Policy of economic and social compromise, or the man behind the state warfare of War Communism. Historians are often swayed in their opinions by their own views of socialism and communism, if they can bear to see a difference at all. On the one hand, when Lenin's initial ideas failed, he was pragmatic enough to adopt new ones, and he wasn't wedded to any theory: he would do what he had to in order to survive. On the other, he called for mass executions, class warfare, concentration camps and Red Terror.

Lenin survived being shot by an assassin, and didn't live a luxurious life. He was not Napoleon, he was not even Kerensky. However, stress and argument had always made him ill (and yes, he was often ill as he was always arguing), and the pressure of running a country exacerbated it. Where he'd once taken time to rest, after 1918 he could take none. His health declined, and between 1922 and 1924 he experienced a series of strokes. Partially paralysed, he had to be prevented from killing himself.

After his second stroke, Lenin, the man who had reshaped Russia, became a prisoner, not of the state but of Stalin. The latter was able to restrict the flow of people and information to Lenin, and a third stroke left him basically unable to speak. He'd managed to write a 'testament' examining the situation, one which was adamant Stalin must not be allowed power, and one which Orland Figes believes shows Lenin, at the end, concluded the revolution had come before Russia was ready.

He died on January 21st, 1924. Stalin had the body put on public show.

Aftermath

Lenin's perversion of socialism, dubbed Marxist-Leninism, became the basis of twentieth century communism and many revolutions across the globe as people followed this example. In this respect, he is one of the most important people of the twentieth century. Was he able to wage a war on his own people because years of exile had divorced him from them? Did he not understand the Russian worker or peasant, seeing them only as pieces in his revolution? How much of his appeal was his drive and determination to act in a revolutionary year so full of dithering? He wasn't eloquent;

his speeches were raging invective which often left him ill. He closed every other aspect of his life off, leaving him a dedicated revolutionary machine, and that was exactly what enabled him to mount a coup in 1917 and hold onto power. And yet, he could change his mind, as he did with Trotsky, a man he'd railed against for years and then forged a strong friendship with. He tolerated opposition from his Bolshevik friends more than Stalin ever would.

Alexander Kerensky

Kerensky was born in 1881, in Simbirsk, to the headmaster of a local school. His father was promoted up in the education system, but not before he had been the headmaster of Lenin, and no, I'm not making that up. Like Lenin, Kerensky studied law, and as he did so in St. Petersburg he became influenced by currents of rebellious thought. He married in 1904, and in 1905 joined the SRs, editing an SR newspaper. He was soon arrested, jailed and exiled, but after only a couple of years he returned to St. Petersburg. So far, so oddly similar to Lenin, but here was where the two men differed.

Kerensky used his law degree, and he used it well, carving out a reputation as a defence lawyer in cases against the government. He worked on the Lena Goldfield Massacre and other high-profile cases, and was elected to the fourth Duma. Here, he found an even wider platform to perform on, and his speeches earned him a following amongst the ordinary workers. Duma membership had other benefits, such as saving him from exile when he triggered a protest over a case of racism.

When World War One began, Kerensky was sceptical, and involved himself in revolutionary activity against the government, but he didn't have any major success and in 1916 went to Finland to recover from health issues. When the revolution came, Kerensky managed to insert himself into the Provisional Government and the Petrograd Soviet, covered in the rest of this book. As the weeks and months passed, Kerensky thought he was a new Napoleon with the answers to Russia's problems, but his adoption of a Tsarist lifestyle was much more successful than his political acts, and he was clinging onto almost no power when Lenin swept him away. While he was brilliant at convincing people, such as soldiers, to fight for him, his powers of persuasion were ephemeral, and people swiftly rejected him when he'd moved on. He stayed in Russia until May 1918 before being sent by SRs and White forces to campaign in Western Europe for intervention in the civil war.

Kerensky's support of allied intervention ceased when the West seemed more interested in monarchists than socialists, and he worked on supporting anti-Bolshevik activity, editing an émigré newspaper, and rounding on political extremists from left and right. A speaking tour of America in 1927 led to a memoir telling his side of the story.

As Europe struggled with what to do about Hitler, Kerensky campaigned for intervention against both Nazism and Communism, while helping Russian dissidents escape from both, and fled the invading Nazi armies only at the last moment. He now made the US home, but even after the war he still campaigned for anti-Communist action, while working to present himself and the Provisional Government in a good light. He died in 1970, having written more memoirs.

New Economic Policy

The Failure of War Communism

Although Lenin had won the Russian Civil War by 1921, he was facing a crisis: the economy was collapsing thanks to the pressures of the war and the corrosive effects of War Communism, the economic system of central government control. The idea of peasants giving up every part of their surplus grain to the rest of the country was always going to be optimistic, and in practice it didn't happen. In fact, it happened so little that Lenin and Trotsky had to use grain requisitioning at gunpoint. War Communism had effectively turned into sending the army to battle the peasants, and millions had risen in rebellion. A third of urban Russians had fled cities to be closer to the origins of food in the country. There were still famines and supply problems and, with the war finished, the five million-strong Red Army was about to decant millions of demobilized soldiers back into this shattered economy. The workers were striking en masse, the peasants only obeying (when they did) because the Reds seemed better than the Whites. It looked like the soldiers would rebel too.

Pragmatic Change and 'Strategic Retreat'

Then they did. The Kronshtadt rebellion of March 1921 saw heroes of the revolution turned against it and needing to be crushed. Lenin decided a more pragmatic approach was required, even if plenty of his fellow Bolsheviks thought War Communism was the system they should stick with permanently. His answer was New Economic Policy. This combined socialist and free market ideas, so while it kept state control of heavy industry, transport and other sectors, it also allowed light industry, retail and most importantly agriculture to change back to private ownership and to operate in a market. Money returned, and the government stopped taking all excess agricultural produce and collected a tax, in kind and then in cash, allowing peasants to sell their surplus for profit. Lenin referred to it as a 'strategic retreat', which would protect the revolution and allow the economy to strengthen for further change. It was an attempt to produce a style of socialism that would work in a peasant state.

New Economic Policy was controversial among Bolsheviks, with some regarding it as a betrayal of the revolution: after all, why was the market coming back? It's no less controversial among historians. On the one hand, the Soviet economy did recover, and the Bolsheviks stayed in power. However, Figes argues in *A People's Tragedy* that it failed because under NEP, peasants would always move away from the Bolshevik regime which would inevitably always have to bloodily reassert control.

The End of NEP

The NEP produced a new class of small businessmen, who were called NEP men. As they benefitted the Bolsheviks argued. Lenin maintained this was a 'temporary' system, but in his mind that could mean over ten years, and lasted only as long as he was alive. Russia's new leader, Stalin, edged out all his opponents by cleverly using issues like the future of NEP as a weapon with which to split them off. In 1928 he ended the NEP in favour of his Five Year Plans and Collectivization, a much more centralized approach. Whether Lenin would have put forward such economic changes, or whether he would have left NEP, we don't know. But, certainly in the short term, the policy was a success when it came to taking a Russian economy broken during world war and civil war, and making it grow again.

Made in the USA
Middletown, DE
16 October 2020